SECOND EDITION

pricing *with* confidence

TEN RULES FOR INCREASING PROFITS AND STAYING AHEAD OF INFLATION

REED K. HOLDEN
JEET MUKHERJEE

WILEY

Published by John Wiley & Sons, Inc., Hoboken, New Jersey.
Published simultaneously in Canada.

For general information on our other products and services or for technical support, please contact our Customer Care Department within the United States at (800) 762-2974, outside the United States at (317) 572-3993 or fax (317) 572-4002.

Wiley also publishes its books in a variety of electronic formats. Some content that appears in print may not be available in electronic formats. For more information about Wiley products, visit our web site at www.wiley.com.

Library of Congress Cataloging-in-Publication Data

Names: Holden, Reed K., author. | Mukherjee, Jeet, author.
Title: Pricing with confidence : ten rules for increasing profits and
    staying ahead of inflation / Reed K. Holden and Jeet Mukherjee.
Description: Second edition. | Hoboken, New Jersey : Wiley, [2023] |
    Includes index.
Identifiers: LCCN 2022028742 (print) | LCCN 2022028743 (ebook) | ISBN
    9781119910183 (cloth) | ISBN 9781119910206 (adobe pdf) | ISBN
    9781119910190 (epub)
Subjects: LCSH: Pricing. | Service industries—Prices.
Classification: LCC HF5416.5 .H647 2023 (print) | LCC HF5416.5 (ebook) |
    DDC 658.8/16—dc23/eng/20220805
LC record available at https://lccn.loc.gov/2022028742
LC ebook record available at https://lccn.loc.gov/2022028743

Cover Design: Wiley
Cover Image: © Pokki/Getty Images

SKY10035849_083022

Contents

Preface

The Inflation Imperative

Inflation—the worst inflation in 40 years—complicates profitability and revenue generation. In short, inflation confounds every aspect of pricing. Readers need another pricing book because very few professionals working today have muscle memory of what pricing in conditions of high inflation demands. The last time inflation was this high was in 1982. How many business leaders and pricing professionals have experience that goes back to the early 1980s? Vanishingly few. It's at this point we realized that despite inflation, business leaders and pricing professionals need resources to help them increase profitability and revenue. Business leaders need resources to help them evolve their organizations to optimize profitability and revenue considering inflation and supply chain instability. The authors of *Pricing with Confidence* accept that we can be part of the solution because over the past three decades, our clients have assured us that we have been true partners in helping them achieve profitable revenue in all pricing conditions.

We became convinced that an inflation edition of *Pricing with Confidence* could help pricing professionals move beyond the noise of that moment and begin working on things over which they actually have control and that this would contribute to the overall success of their respective firms. We've seen many professionals become bogged down in the details of fancy tactics and technologies and miss the simple truths of what needs to be done.

While inflation complicates every aspect of the pricing process, a key theme of *Pricing With Confidence: Second Edition* is that it's possible for readers to focus on controlling what they can as inflation rises and the economy rises and falls right alongside it. This edition of the book represents nothing less than a master class on pricing leadership through inflationary times. A key lesson is that pricing leaders must decide: sacrifice margins by absorbing the impacts of inflation or refocus their business model. Every variable in the business model—pricing, inventories, adjusting the product line, separating unprofitable customers, narrowing your customer base, and selecting your customers far more carefully—must be considered in the glaring light of inflation.

The authors of the second edition resonated with the reality that this generation of working pricing professionals has no direct experience working in the context of inflation and dramatic supply chain disruptions. Our book, we are convinced, will offer pricing leaders a roadmap for overseeing a paradigm shift in the organizations' business models. Such a shift conditions the psychology and motivation of every pricing leader to respond quickly to the challenges of inflation.

Because inflation is such a volatile force, the book argues that it's imperative for leaders to make pricing decisions sooner and better. Such decisions (e.g., shrinking the workforce or exiting cash-inefficient businesses) are wrenching in the best of times. There is little time for equivocation with rising inflation. The optimum response to inflation may be to shrink a firm's size to make them more focused and efficient. This act, while seemingly counterintuitive, can actually grow revenue and profits. The very analytics and metrics that leaders previously relied on—think margins, cash flow, gross revenue growth, and market share gain—will likely have to be reprioritized.

Our bottom line is that we knew we could help people like you manage pricing better. This inflation edition of *Pricing with Confidence* cuts through the misconceptions of pricing in inflationary times to deliver the proven truths that help make companies nimble enough in their pricing disciplines to generate incremental uplift. This second edition anticipates that there will be various business "shocks" along the way. Of course, readers of the second edition will find practical responses to those events. Our main goal is for this edition of *Pricing with Confidence* to provide you with the tools and resources required to build an organization that executes well in the face of so much volatility. So, here goes. Hope you enjoy the ride.

Reed Holden
Jeet Mukherjee
Concord, MA
September 2022

Acknowledgments

Reed Holden is fortunate to have had an abundance of good teachers over the years. The late Professor Paul Berger at Boston University was one. He took the time to teach not only the techniques and practical applications of analytics, but more important, how to think about them simply. Those lessons continue to serve us well through the years. Reed is especially grateful to David Rogers, professor of management at Babson College, for his teachings on analytics, and Kevin J. Clancy for his pragmatic approach to the complex world of consumer research.

We would each like to thank the Holden Advisors team who have helped us push forward the theory of pricing and selling and focus on our primary mission of helping clients obtain more revenue and profits. With gratitude, we also acknowledge Adnan Akbari, Ali Crist, Heidi Hager, Aaron Fransen, Mike Cannestra, Emily Lawson, Adele McClean, Amy Gribbel, Pete Morelli, Laura Miller, Monica McCarty, Mechell Hoxie, Patrick McCullough, Bonnie Plapper, Ellen Quackenbush, Lori Rybaski, Teng Yang, Tracy Dent, Becky Sansoterra, Kris Olinger, Travis Umpleby, Derek Neal, and Karen Kunz. Thanks, also, to Chris Mitchell for making Backbone a reality in our business.

There are two people who deserve special mention for having done an outstanding job of moving the firm forward despite the turmoil of the past few years. Brian Doyle has built and leads a team of high-performance individuals during an extraordinary time of growth while meeting new challenges with our clients. Carolyn Holden is the visionary leader who helps us pivot in these times of change. She continues to drive our firm to the future with a push and a smile, and her work coordinating and editing this book helped us get the job done.

We've built our book on pricing on the shoulders of many great colleagues over the years. Tom Nagle gave us the first nudge into the world of pricing with his writings and when he formed Strategic Pricing Group. The late Dan Nimer's voice continues to echo in our minds when we think about value. The contributions of Mark Burton, my pricing partner and coauthor on the first edition of *Pricing with Confidence,* continue to influence my understanding of price discipline. We appreciate Professor Gerald Smith of the Carroll School of Management, Boston College for his contributions to the fields of product and brand management specialization as well as his friendship and support over the years.

Numerous clients and business partners have helped to forge our thoughts as well. We'd like to mention a few: Gene Zelek, Lynn Guinn, Neil Wilson, Mark James, Bob Vezeau, Andy Slusher, Rob Krugman, Andrew Fisher, Ken Beyer, Randy Kobat, Debi Prickette, David Ivester, Michael McNulty, Brian Coe, Joe Muchnick, Joel Rickman, Naser Hamdi, Mike Bromley, Lisa Nelson, Greg Creel, and Ted Hinz. We'd like to give a special thanks to Rudy Ploder, who is a visionary value-based leader and a true strategic partner to our firm.

Thanks from both authors go also to the editorial staff at Wiley: Jessica Filippo, our editorial champion, Richard Narramore, executive editor, Business Books, and Debbie Schindlar, managing editor.

This is the fourth book we've delivered with John Kador as our team's developmental editor. Throughout what can be an arduous process, John has provided a steady stream of support and kind words, not to mention his great writing. We're lucky to have him on the team and are grateful for his willingness to continue to partner with us. Kimberly Railsback, our crayon evangelist, works her magic with graphics, book cover art, logos, and icons with a unique and talented eye.

Reed would like to acknowledge his mother, Dorothy E. Holden, who was born exactly 100 years before this second edition. A further round of heartfelt appreciation goes to his children and their spouses, Rebecca and Patrick McCullough, Mark Holden and Lauren Dempsey; and his grandchildren, Hudson, Carter, and Nolan McCullough, who provide immense joy.

Jeet would like to acknowledge Reed Holden, for getting him started on his value-based journey over 20 years ago. The impact Reed has had on Jeet's career is immeasurable. Jeet also appreciates Carolyn Holden and Brian Doyle for their trust and guidance. Personally, he thanks his mother, Krishna Basu, and sister, Poonam Basu, for their unconditional love; his wife, Kelly Mukherjee, and kids, Neel, Aidan, and Kyle, for giving his life meaning; his cousin, Bipasha Mukhopadhyay, for showing her love through food; and Jeet's chosen family of Chris Payne, Yas Rahimi, Richard Rucker, and Greg James for always being there without question.

Introduction: Getting Used to Supply Chain and Cost Turbulence

Inflation and supply chain disruptions have emerged as perhaps the most stubborn challenges brought about by the COVID-19 pandemic and then exacerbated by world events. News reports proclaim that inflation rates are the highest in four decades. It's true. In 2022, inflation, as measured by the Consumer Price Index, showed the largest year-to-year increase since 1982, according to the U.S. Bureau of Labor Statistics' seasonally adjusted data. Contributing to inflation are supply chain bottlenecks including disruptions in intermediate goods, semiconductor shortages, shipping interruptions, and labor shortages.

The good news is that the world is getting the coronavirus under control. The unwelcome news is that inflation and supply chain disruptions spawned by the pandemic will take years to stabilize. While lockdowns and business shutdowns are relics of the past, businesses face a post-pandemic future that is filled with challenges. The consequences of these challenges are now being felt by entrepreneurs and business leaders all over the world.

No matter what service sector you do business in or what industrial sector you operate in, inflation makes it imperative that business leaders make the right strategic decisions. Inflation complicates every aspect of running a business. Left unmanaged, inflation will quickly render profitable businesses marginal and decimate the product and revenue mix that in pre-inflationary times returned handsome profits.

The Importance of Leadership

Price success starts with an unclouded vision articulated by the CEO. Discipline and patience are next along with a tolerance for ambiguity. The results materialize after resistance and vetting from different stakeholders. When Parker Hannifin's then CEO Donald Washkewicz (he retired in 2016) took on the pricing beast, the company improved net income by over 500% and return on net income by 300%. What was Washkewicz's secret to success? It started with discipline. As the CEO, he took a focused effort to acknowledge that at least with some of its products, Parker Hannifin provided value it was not capturing.

The biggest problem Parker Hannifin executives faced was persuading company managers and sales professionals that they would benefit from the new pricing mantra. In the words of one executive, the company had to "reprogram the company's management DNA." One consequence: the company shifted to align pricing with that recognized value. The company developed the tools to help hungry salespeople effectively confront customers who were clamoring for lower prices. Washkewicz had the confidence to act on the basis of Parker Hannifin's self-professed mission statement: to be a supplier of high-value products and services. He used that knowledge to price with confidence. The Parker Hannifin sales teams took confidence from the CEO's direction and discipline. Results quickly showed the promise of starting with value and demonstrating to customers the benefits they derived from being Parker Hannifin customers. Since his retirement, the firm still has a core value of "quality solutions on time" and "ease of doing business," which in part continue to support strong earnings and revenue growth.

The CEO or president is usually the ideal executive to continually sponsor changes because, make no mistake about it, resistance to change is real and only a champion at the very top can pull the levers to drive change. Salespeople and their managers must know with absolute certainty that there is a place where the buck stops and attempts to go over the head of the change agent will be fruitless.

With this mindset, companies are ready to identify where and how certain products and services are superior to those of their competitors. Then someone is directed to lead the charge in recognizing that value, quantifying it, putting it into a competitive context, and executing it through an engaged salesforce. Armed with demonstrable value, salespeople can start to feel good about what they are selling. When a customer says there is no value, the salespeople remember who they are, what company they work for, and they begin to price with confidence using value conversations to find the win-win with customers.

As we've collaborated with firms over the years, we've found that for Pricing with Confidence to work, it takes a diligent leader to sponsor change, take control, and empower UVPF (Understand Value, Price Fairly), which is a core process within the organization. That leader may be the CEO as in the case of Parker Hannifin, or it could be the CFO or division president. In all cases, it's best if the senior executive leading the change reports directly to the CEO. That direct line of reporting sends the message that the CEO has the back of the executive leading the change. There must be no doubt among the departments that appealing unpopular pricing changes to the CEO is an effective strategy.

One of our first pricing training programs was with Intel. The semiconductor leader had an engaged senior leadership team but, just as important, they had a VP of Pricing who reported directly to the CEO. Intel made training a key element of the growth of their team and kept value and competitive price strategy at the core of what they offered. Evolving between a skim strategy for emerging technologies and a neutral strategy when the competition, in this case AMD, entered with matching products, Intel also used innovation of newer technologies as a key element of its growth targets for revenue and profitability. Today, Intel is one of the largest chip makers in the world with an astounding 30% net income.

Building the Value-Based Pricing Team

One of the most frequent questions we are asked is where, organizationally, the pricing team should reside in a company. The usual choices are within the marketing, finance, product management, or sales functions. The basic question is what do you want the pricing department to prioritize. Putting the pricing team in any of these areas means that they will comport themselves in line with how the departments are measured. Pricing within the sales organization likely says they will be more revenue focused; in finance they will be more invested in cost and margin; in marketing they will be more fixated on branding and promotion. If they land in product management, sales tend to focus on products versus the overall solution a company can offer. An effective pricing organization should focus on all of these and then some. Pricing is a team sport, but to be successful, pricing needs to focus on generating profit for the firm (Rule One).

Start with the End Goals

What would success for a pricing organization look like, especially given today's economic climate? We went out and asked this question of various leaders, mostly C-Suite leaders from assorted vertical industry segments. From these conversations, four key themes surfaced:

- Stop the bleeding
- Increase speed
- Manage risk
- Find insights that matter

Let's look at each of these themes:

1. **Stop the bleeding.** Undisciplined pricing practices are a profit killer. To stop the bleeding, discounting goes under a microscope and practices are put in place to stop profit leakages. One image in your microscope is your customers. We spoke to Andrew Fisher, founder and CEO of Myriad360, a West Deptford, New Jersey–based provider of IT infrastructure and solutions. During the pandemic, Myriad360 purposefully went from serving approximately 600 customers to 240 active accounts. The company purposefully fired its unprofitable customers. "The most unprofitable customers were taking up valuable resources and making it difficult to properly service high-value customers," Fisher said. The end result for the IT solutions company was a smaller revenue base, but higher profitability, higher customer satisfaction, and higher employee engagement.

2. **Increase speed** refers to making pricing-related decisions quickly based on market volatility. One client has a goal of "sub-second" price changes because they deal with raw materials, and the cost of those are constantly changing in these inflationary times. Speed of price execution is vital for their survival. Automation is fueling their speed. Any time companies can automate their pricing processes, especially for the long tail of customers, the more time and resources they can spend on more strategic customers, and they will continue to profit through inflationary times.

3. **Manage risk.** While every leader regarded managing risk from their individual perspectives of the markets they served, they all came to the same two conclusions. The first is that every pricing organization must make managing risk an imperative. The second is that diversification is the number one most effective response to minimizing risk. That includes diversification of markets, customers, products, solutions, and even supply chains. The CEO of a major IT manufacturer detailed how the company added more countries to their supply chain processes to mitigate the risks during the pandemic. Another response is customer customization, bespoke offerings, services, and pricing. With the cost of data storage coming down and our ability to do analytics in micro-seconds on large data sets, the world of customization is much easier to execute. This also leads to more collaborative go-to-market strategies with channel partners.

4. **Find insights that matter.** Don't wait for perfection and don't waste time preparing large, complicated reports. Instead, focus on creating insights at the points of need that are easily actionable. Too many times companies produce reports that are not actionable and, worse, they consume unproductive cycles of time where people argue over numbers and leaders ask to see the data cut in distinct ways to make them look better. We worked with one firm that had a team of 60 professionals consolidating data from multiple platforms to provide insights on pricing. By leveraging an outside data facilitator, we were able to provide actionable insights in a timely manner at a fraction of the cost.

Understand the Capabilities Needed

Based on these end-goals, a successful pricing organization is strategic and has the capability to influence other parts of the organization. They can't be only an operational function where they are changing prices based on what other departments are telling them to do. Nor can they be just a price optimization shop where they sit in IT and manage a software solution that often misses relevant issues inside and outside of the firm.

Here are ten pricing-related competencies that every company should master if they wish to achieve these end goals. This list aligns with the Pricing Leadership Framework outlined in Chapter 1 (Price for Profit).

1. Understand the customer and value
2. Understand the competitors
3. Align pricing to company strategy
4. Create and communicate offerings that align with value
5. Set list price
6. Govern the price
7. Refresh price
8. Employ analytics to track the proper metrics
9. Invest in analytics to create insights
10. Productize: build, enhance, maintain processes with insights that lead to measurable actions

While most of the capabilities are self-explanatory, there are two elements typically lacking in our clients. One is understanding the customer and value. Often the sales leader will tell us that they know their customer really well and will point to an example like, "I went to their kids' graduation party!" Personal relationships with customers are fine, but what we mean here is an intimate understanding of the customers' business—how they generate revenue, cut costs, or mitigate risk by using your solution. This is not a static activity. Customers change, innovate, and explore new markets, so your solutions need to be in step with their evolving needs. Especially in a volatile market, this understanding is the basis for all pricing activities and is a critical capability.

The second capability often missing in clients is the ability to productize. It's one thing to create insights using analytics, but insights are useless until they are implemented. Productizing your insights by building them into key processes is vital for sustained profitability. With one client, we found that an open quote had a higher likelihood of closure if the customer was "touched" at least three times. "Touched" means everything from a salesperson's call to the customer to an opened email reminding a customer of the open quote. It's best to automate such insights. We designed an automated email campaign where customers with at least two touches were automatically emailed for that third touch. Just this simple process doubled the close rates of open quotes.

Support the Value Leader

Senior leadership has the challenging assignment of making sure that everyone in the organization keeps their focus on improving and better leveraging value for customers. To support the value leader, the president or CEO should understand the interconnectivity of departmental activities and implement metrics that track to optimal results for the integrated team rather than a silo approach. The leader should make certain that the approach and process involve everyone in the company. When senior managers have a value focus, they can implement effective controls that begin to look at overall quality of output in production and customer retention. Sales managers can help salespeople focus on more profitable business rather than any business. New goals can evaluate how marketing managers improve the effectiveness of salespeople and how that turns into increased margins and profits for the firm.

There are a number of short-term steps that can facilitate the customer value process and add revenue and profits fairly quickly to the company. Start by asking senior sales and marketing vice presidents how their people create value with their activities. Follow up with even more specific questions:

- Do you have a market segment where salespeople can focus on high-value prospects?
- Does marketing provide the right value messages to make the salespeople's jobs easier?
- Do you have insights that can be shared into how your products and services perform relative to the competition?
- Do you have insights in the performance difference, and can it convert to financial benefits for customers?

What can you do with your offering, positioning, and seller negotiating skills to improve closing rates without using price as the primary lever?

- Are the right salespeople focused on the right accounts?
- Are sales reps trained and motivated to focus on transactions with price buyers only or do they have the skills to drive value with relationship and value-oriented customers?
- How well is your entire team equipped to deal with the aggressive poker playing we see in many deals today?

These questions will drive the company to an outside-in value culture. This will provide the foundation to confidently limit price-only negotiations. Everyone in the organization must be grounded in the reality that they really do provide value to customers and that it's their obligation to leverage that value with fair pricing.

Avoid Urgency

The biggest problem facing business leaders from CEOs to sales professionals is supply chain disruption. Plant closings and labor shortages resulting from the pandemic are decimating the abilities of suppliers to meet the needs of their customers. On the heels of the pandemic, the invasion of Ukraine sent oil prices reeling. The consequential economic sanctions against Russia have already played out in higher prices at the gasoline pump. The disruptions to raw materials needed for supply chains will add to shortages and inflationary pressures. That's causing consumers and companies alike to hoard critical supplies, further exacerbating the problem.

What's an executive (pricing or otherwise) to do? Here's our first piece of advice, and it is perhaps the most important one to start with. What should you do right now? Take a breath. Avoid urgency. Because when many executives respond with snap decisions to a business problem, they invariably react to the wrong problem.

Ken Beyer is CEO of Atlanta-based Transportation Insight Holding Company, a $3.2 billion enterprise that helps client shippers engineer efficient supply chain networks. Beyer believes that the market volatility that we are seeing today will persist for at least a few years. "The supply chain is broken," Beyer said. "We've all noticed bare shelves in stores, felt the effects of rising inflation, and struggled to forecast changing demands. Moreover, shipping costs continue to rise, capacity remains tight, ships are trapped outside of ports, and uncertainty is a dark cloud hanging over businesses." Much of the problem is because legacy supply chains were not built for ecommerce; they simply were not ready to manage the spike in ecommerce volume created by the pandemic as consumers shopped from home. "This also created a movement of labor from consumers picking up goods from brick and mortars to a new labor market for deliveries," Beyer noted. This new labor market created opportunities for new delivery services and shifted labor from warehouses, loading docks, and retail to home deliveries, as an example. This fundamental shift was one of many factors in the labor shortage.

A number of business decisions are made tactically and without sufficient analytical foundation. That is, the response is focused on only a part of the problem using the tools and levers at hand. The results are often sub-optimal in that they don't address the real problem and they spawn unintended consequences and second order effects that often make the problem worse.

The problem for pricing professionals today is twofold. First, pricing professionals are called on to provide leadership in the most turbulent times in four decades. Second—and this is the real problem that the following chapters will address—is that executives today simply do not have the experience or muscle memory to operate in these most challenging of environments. The result is that some leaders often panic and do more harm than good by making reactionary decisions that fail to consider the total pricing environment.

A brief example of how one of our clients navigated the challenges of the pandemic serves to demonstrate the strategic benefits of the practices described in this book. Shortly after the pandemic hit, many of our clients began receiving calls from their customer procurement people asking for price cuts. We advised them to change the conversation from price cuts to how a closer strategic relationship could assure them of a reliable supply chain. We'll talk about this practice in Rule Ten: Deploy Three Practices to Increase Profits.

In the middle of all the alarm about supply chain problems from the pandemic, we were working with one of our clients to better understand where competitors were priced (higher) and why customers bought some of their products (because they had to). That led to a doubling of price. Of course, it took more than just that. Using the pricing discipline we helped instill over the years throughout this client's organization, the leaders were in an excellent position to confront the strategic supply chain issues now looming before them.

It was possible because, with the help of the lessons described in this book, the client had over the years developed a fearless, forward-looking leadership team up and down the organization, confident it had the tools and skills to manage inflation fears and supply chain interruptions. Elsewhere in the book, we will describe more specifically how this client prospered while others struggled, for now here's the view from 10,000 feet.

The client leveraged every one of the ten rules this book establishes for achieving profits in inflationary times. The pricing discipline instilled throughout the pricing and sales teams had succeeded in Kicking the Discounting Habit (Rule Three). They had established sufficient confidence in the value they delivered to Build Your Selling Backbone (Rule Nine) and were using innovation (Rule Six) to Build Give-Gets Muscle (Rule Eight). They were already proficient at execution (Rule Two) and were in the process of establishing an internal group with responsibility for overall strategy of the division (Rule Five).

Briefly, that describes the framework this book successfully exploited by our clients and available to readers and leaders committed to achieving the primary revenue and profitability objectives of their businesses despite inflation and supply chain turbulence. The framework encompasses ten rules or practices that, in coordination, set out a strategic road map to guide business leaders and entrepreneurs. These objectives are to grow the firm's revenues and profits. We believe that if pricing professionals diligently follow the practices described in the following pages, they will be optimally situated to safeguard the revenue and profitability goals their businesses have established despite inflationary complications.

How This Book Is Organized: Ten Rules for Increasing Revenue and Profitability

The heart of Pricing with Confidence is ten rules. Each rule is a reminder to all stakeholders of what is needed to grow both profits and revenue in increasingly inflationary, competitive, price-oriented markets. With one chapter dedicated to each rule, readers will get a detailed explanation of each rule supported by multiple examples and actual case histories directly from our playbook.

We are pleased that you have continued reading this far into the Introduction. As you have noted, the Introduction lays out the case for why pricing in inflationary and supply-constrained conditions requires a new understanding of strategic pricing. We especially recommend the Introduction for readers who are not yet persuaded that high inflation and related supply chain turbulence fundamentally recalibrates established pricing practices.

Price for Profits. The pricing mantra of Pricers and Leaders should always be to "price for profits." Companies that successfully manage price over the past few decades have deployed this mantra with tremendous success. Rule One reminds us, when business leaders lose sight of this truth, even temporarily, it results in difficulties that are not easily reversed. Price for Profits is the lodestone of the book, hence its place at number one in the sequence of ten rules. It requires learning from the past and taking initiative. Business leaders cannot Price for Profits on a hunch. Analytics are indispensable, as are quality metrics. Like all simple truths, the operation of Rule One is not difficult to comprehend. Nor is it too difficult to execute *if* there is a universal commitment on the part of everyone in the business to—primarily—Price for Profits.

An Ounce of Execution Is Better Than a Pound of Planning. The main takeaway is that a bias for action is one of the hallmarks of effective pricing leaders. While developing a strategy is important, too many businesses squander opportunities by indulging in strategic planning that is obsolete by the time it is finished. Here's a better way. Having good execution systems and people who follow them is an especially important rule for pricing in inflationary and turbulent times. Rule Two discusses where in the corporate hierarchy a value-based pricing organization should reside. Some of the skills associated with Rule Two include how to change sales and customer expectations, how to use analytics to, among other things, identify unprofitable customers, and when to fire them.

Kick the Discounting Habit. Price discounting is an addiction that is entrenched in many organizations. As with any addiction, the discounting habit is tough to break cold turkey. The best way to dislodge any deep-seated attitude is to replace it with another. A bit of arrogance, feeling good about the value of your products and services, and why the price is the price provides the confidence needed to kick the discounting habit. The chapter begins by describing the problem with discounting, offering practical tips to kick the discounting habit, and analyzing how desperation during inflation can cause pricing professionals to do the wrong thing.

Know Your Value. It's true the customer has the last word on defining value, but that doesn't mean the business is silent on the matter. Businesses establish value when they do such an excellent job of identifying what matters most to customers and then delivering it consistently so that it earns repeat business. When business leaders fail to establish business value, they squander revenue, lose profits, and fritter away market share as their clients find more favorable offerings. Customer value can be heightened when companies find ways to align their core competencies with their customers' primary go-to-market efforts. Without understanding value, you are doing business in a very dark cave. Understanding the value you and your firm create for your customers is like flooding the cave with light.

Confidence in negotiation requires confidence in pricing. Confidence in pricing derives from an enterprise-wide understanding of and belief in the value the business delivers to customers. Customers buy your products and services to achieve value. Understanding and living that value is a key to successful pricing.

Strategy Sets the Direction. Choosing the right pricing is dependent on market conditions, product life cycle, and understanding customers' use cases for your products and services. If the tactics of pricing determine how much to charge for a particular product or service, then product pricing strategy determines whether to price higher, lower, or equal to competition. The main takeaway of this chapter is that pricing strategy should be simple and understood by all, especially the pricing professionals and the salesforce.

Complex pricing strategies may look good on paper but implementing them becomes impractical. Strategy should be simple and understood by all, especially your pricing people and your salesforce. Complex strategies get in the way of that understanding. In this chapter, you will learn why many approaches fail, compare three basic pricing strategies and when to use them, and discover a pricing strategy focused on capital intensive businesses as well as for businesses offering software and information products.

Innovate for Growth. Innovation provides the engine of profitable growth and is far more effective than lower prices in establishing a sustainable competitive advantage. Businesses that don't evolve their products in services will fail to meet the evolving needs of customers and leave an opening for competitors. Successful companies are continually looking for ways to improve their product and service offerings. That means smart companies innovate for growth, relentlessly price for profits, understand the basics of a good offering structure, and use solutions and services to create price leverage.

Understand Your Market. If you are going to succeed with pricing on any level, you must have a clear understanding of how customers and competitors are going to respond to whatever pricing initiative you undertake. In other words, you need to understand that the market is a complex interaction of many players all pursuing their self-interests. If you don't have that comprehensive understanding of how markets operate—particularly your market—and invest the time and resources in developing that understanding, your efforts will backfire. The chapter looks at some elements of basic game theory, asking if you are better at playing checkers or chess. The chapter also introduces The Elasticity Tattoo, defines "derived demand," and details the obstacles to using pricing to drive growth.

Build Your Give-Get Muscle. Give-Gets are little gems and the best way to protect price. Salespeople need trade-offs and negotiation tactics, otherwise they continue to be a big source of price leakage. Too often, they just give on price. There's a better way. Negotiating with product and service features as trade-offs are a better way to blunt the poker playing tactics of customers and protect the value of those products and services. This chapter gives readers indispensable tools to use offering structure to win at the negotiating table. It describes the importance of internal alignment on executing Give-Gets. Some of the practices described in Chapter 8 include bundling and how strong fences protect value.

Build Your Selling Backbone to Add Profits. Backbone (the chief support of a system or organization; figuratively, strength in the face of adversity) provides resilience to your team as the assaults on your pricing strategy mount. The main thrust of Rule Nine is that you can't demonstrate and prove your value if you don't have Backbone. Confidence in negotiation requires confidence in pricing. Confidence in pricing derives from knowing the value of your products or services as perceived by the customer. That requires knowing your customers' requirements, how your solution will make an impact, and the confidence to stand behind the price.

Backbone also requires knowing the tricks your customers use to get you to drop prices and how to interrupt the cultures that default to deep discounting of products. In such cultures, managers believe that there is no other way. Regardless of product, competition, or geographic location, firms that Sell with Backbone sell more, do it profitably, and actually have a bit more fun.

Deploy Three Practices to Increase Profits. This chapter reviews three practical ways to dramatically increase profits. The secrets include the powerful concept of UVPF (Understand Value, Price Fairly), how to play better poker, price like the airlines to better leverage resources, and how to increase profits in inflationary times.

Price with Confidence—The Journey. The conclusion of the book wraps together all of the elements of the ten rules to provide a roadmap for readers to move forward. Themes of the conclusion include building the team, the importance of leadership, and a discussion of the central question, Who owns value?

Now, let's begin with Rule One.

CHAPTER 1

Rule One

Price for Profit

Inflation complicates every aspect of pricing. Rule One is about using price to increase profits. Profits result when an organization understands how their products and services create value for their customers. Higher levels of profit come when a firm sets a fair price based on that value and executes those prices through a salesforce that is prepared to capture, not discount the set prices with customers.

For the first time in decades, persistent inflation has become an urgent short-term consideration for companies around the world. Our view is that while inflation certainly complicates every aspect of pricing, it also represents an ideal opportunity to make long-overdue changes to pricing practices. For that reason, struggling with short-term inflation may have some long-term benefits.

Inflation has propelled the issue of pricing from the backroom to the boardroom. For all the pain it imposes, inflation actually has an unseen benefit. It's that the attention of C-suite business executives will never be more focused on pricing than it is right now. C-Suite leaders are acutely attentive to the unavoidable fact that inflation has an unforgiving impact on the profits of companies that fail to manage it with agility. When input costs rise drastically, an enterprise's profits will take a dive unless it can quickly pass along price increases, and when it comes to inflation, nimbleness is the imperative.

Most analysts agree on two things. One, that the rate of inflation growth—and the related pain of supply chain volatility—is the highest it has been in more than four decades. Two, that inflation is persistent and that it represents a long-term systemic challenge to businesses large and small. While the Consumer Price Index (CPI) as reported by The Commerce Department recently topped 8.5%—the highest since 1981—we are actually more focused on the less well-known U.S. Producer Price Index. That index, measuring inflation for processed goods for intermediate demand, rose by 24.4% in 2021, the index's largest calendar-year increase since 1974. The International Monetary Fund's All Commodity Price Index increased by 49% in the same 12 months. The bottom line is that inflation-driven supply chain volatility, compounded by the COVID-19 pandemic labor shortages, intensifies the pricing pressures on businesses in every sector and those pressures will not soon recede.

When the Tide Goes Out

The persistent global inflation we are experiencing today exposes a limitation of most B2B pricing practices. "You only find out who is swimming naked when the tide goes out," is a nugget of wisdom attributed to Warren Buffett, the most successful investor in American history. What the Oracle of Omaha means by this observation is that you really can't tell whose investing strategy works or appreciate the risks that businesses are taking when markets are performing well. Only when markets are challenged by adverse conditions can we discriminate between those who are smart and those who are just lucky.

While Buffet's aphorism chiefly applies to investors, it is relevant to the general pricing practices of businesses large and small. It's no secret that virtually every business tolerates legacy pricing practices they know to be sub-optimal. In a stable and flourishing market, these inefficiencies were mostly tolerated. But when confronted by rapidly rising input costs combined with supply chain volatility, the limitations of legacy pricing practices suddenly can no longer be ignored.

C-suite leaders around the world are seeing that inflation is forcing the tide to recede. Many are rightly concerned about what their stakeholders will see. When inflationary pressures cause costs to increase at the same time that supply chain disruptions soften demand, certain pricing practices turn out to be too slow, too lax, and too undifferentiated.

All is not lost. The practices prescribed by this book will help you modernize your firm's pricing practices to best leverage the challenges of persistent inflation. Inflation gives you opportunities to raise prices. No customer welcomes price increases, but end-users tend to be receptive to pricing upticks backed by a well-articulated and robust rationale. For now, remember that the more your price increase can accurately reflect value and the true cost increases of your products and services, the better you will protect the profits of the firm.

Costs Are Going Up

The best signal that you're in inflationary times is that your costs are going up. Maybe you can see those increases coming from reading the trade and business press. Those costs can rise due to supply shortage, production problems, or random shocks to the delivery chain from weather, for example. The trick is to have a system in place to recognize that inflation is coming, and you will need to pass those costs on to your customers. Delaying that sequence will cut into and possibly eliminate your profits.

Since most companies have a wide range of products, cost increases can have varying impacts on the need to increase prices. Many firms try to average out those cost increases with a uniform price increase across all products. The problem with doing that is when you have a competitor that increases prices on specific products or product groups to more accurately reflect their true cost increase, you will be at a competitive disadvantage with your prices. That's because the products that have a higher cost increase than the price increase will sell more and the products that have a lower cost increase than the price increase will sell less, thus undermining the profits of the firm and providing sales opportunities to those competitors.

Managers around the world worry more about revenue than profits. Many incentive systems are still based on growing revenue. These models assume that a combination of reductions in costs and efficiencies in operations will boost profits. In the best of circumstances, these promised reductions and efficiencies make an impact only once. Eventually, cost declines level out, and efficiencies reach their limit. The inevitable result is that profits decline.

Pricing executives are often the protector of profits for the firm. We all know that this is easier said than done. It takes strength, persistence, and a lot of thought to protect profits in a sales ecosystem that often works counter to those needs. In this chapter, we'll talk about a more successful pricing structure and the steps necessary to make it sustainable.

Three Necessary Adjustments

The businesses that will thrive in inflationary conditions will adjust their pricing strategies in three fundamental ways to cultivate the necessary speed, agility, and discipline to respond quickly to an endlessly volatile environment.

- **Rapid Response.** In order to avoid margin decreases, businesses need to be able to adjust their prices quickly when costs rise. Commercial teams must be able to quickly set new prices as conditions change and roll them out with discipline.

- **Enforce Discipline.** Businesses often tolerate lax enforcement of discount policies when economic conditions are favorable. Strategic exceptions (what we call discounting concessions) are never the optimal practice, but a certain permissiveness is forgivable. Inflation is unforgiving of such practices. The only bulwark against resistance to price increases is the ability to demonstrate how the product or service in question delivers market-ready value.

- **Systematize Pricing.** Inflation-responsive pricing requires businesses to increase the cadence of price changes. We've seen companies roll out systems to reprice quarterly, monthly, or even daily. The price changes must be nuanced, as well. That means avoiding simplistic, across-the-board price increases. Rather, businesses must be able to deploy a spectrum of differentiated increases tailored by the value each product delivers to each customer situation on a timely basis.

Problems with a Revenue Focus

One of the most destructive myths of business, simply stated, is "If you worry about the sales, profits will take care of themselves." The myth encourages managers to lower prices for the sake of increasing sales. The problem is that this myth will eventually lead to consequences precisely the opposite of what they promise.

What renders this a business myth is the unstated assumption behind it. The assumption is that product or service delivery teams will benefit with increased volume. This mistaken perception causes managers to initiate pricing decisions (usually a discount) to increase revenue that eventually leads to the decline of profits and, in the cases of mature markets, loss of market share and revenue.

Salespeople usually honor this myth by their zeal to close. Their incentives are carefully designed to drive them to close an order, even if that means giving up some or even all the profit. Senior managers add to the problem with their short-term focus on monthly or quarterly revenue numbers and their willingness to sacrifice profits through lower prices to achieve quota. The problem isn't with the people, it's with the incentive and management culture that encourages them to discount.

The myth exposes pricing in the trenches, the moment when a deal seems to be in jeopardy because of price. In the trenches, it's difficult to have confidence and hold the line on your prices, or to know when to confidently walk away from a sale. It's so difficult that many managers make decisions that may or may not increase sales while still undermining profits.

Navigate Inflation's Challenges

How can B2B business leaders help their commercial teams navigate through the challenges of inflation and supply chain volatility? The automatic response—that the CEO's actions must primarily protect profits—is not complete. While inflation certainly has implications for profitability, business leaders must contend with a wide range of stakeholders to think in much wider terms. This chapter begins a process that leads business leaders to answer that question. Like the formulation of any strategy, the process starts by asking questions:

- What price increases will customers accept?
- How should we represent and implement price increases in an inflationary environment?

- In what places will end-users perceive our value in this new environment?
- How can we create partnerships and strategic mindsets that see inflation as a common concern?
- Where can we help procurement leaders change the conversation away from price?
- How can we present our products, services, and experiences to deliver this value?
- What capabilities will we need to increase the company's resilience and control costs?
- What is the fastest way to reinforce stretched and fractured supply chains?
- How can we establish a vision, set priorities, and organize to direct all this activity?

The CEO is an organization's ultimate integrator. Our experience into the behaviors and mindsets of excellent CEOs shows the pivotal role that chief executives play in setting a clear direction, aligning the organization, managing stakeholders, and serving as "motivator in chief."

The best CEOs act boldly, of course, but also operate from core mindsets that often belie the classic image of the hard-charging executive: they approach important decisions by listening first, treat "soft" culture topics as a hard material advantage, empower employees, and ask questions constantly. Pricing for profits is the ultimate objective. The challenge is that many leaders underestimate the deep level of cross-organizational change needed to make this approach stick.

Consider the benefits to a business when managers get enthusiastic about value and start an initiative to move to profit-based pricing. Their early results attract the notice of other leaders, and the initiative is distributed across the organization. The goal of profit-based pricing becomes institutionalized.

Competitive Disadvantage in Your Costs

When managers average costs, it puts them at a competitive disadvantage when making pricing moves against those competitors that don't. This is because some business opportunities look less profitable than they in actuality are. The companies that look at incremental costs will have a much truer picture of the profit coming from any piece of potential business.

The ability to measure and manage incremental costs is especially important for professional services companies such as consulting firms, accounting firms, software companies, and law practices. Let's look at an example of the problem of averaging costs and how they play out in a decentralized corporation with a number of large divisions.

At Division A, the decision was to calculate incremental costs; at Division B, the decision was to fully allocate costs. Over time, this company began shifting most production to Division A, the incrementally costed facility, because their costs appeared lower. The problem was that Division B had extensive fixed investments in plant and equipment. Once Division A began producing products costed incrementally, it actually caused more sales orders to move to their division and led to the dramatic underutilization and losses in Division B. The net result was the demise of the entire firm!

The capacity costs of people and/or of fixed facilities for service companies such as professional services firms tend to be a larger portion of their cost structure than corresponding costs for manufacturing companies. Those costs tend to be fixed over the short-term, especially if people are not going to be separated when utilization is low. Furthermore, unused human capacity is volatile. Just like the value of an unfilled airline seat goes to zero the instant the airplane door closes, the value of a lost day of untapped human capacity to drive revenue and profits evaporates forever.

Costing systems will either help you or hurt you if your pricing purpose is to increase profits. They do that by either preventing or allowing you to accept business that increases the overall profits of the company. Many managers are aware of this approach and its importance but avoid it because they worry that salespeople may start discounting deals down to the level of the incremental costs and all of their business will migrate there. Their concerns are justified.

Fortunately, there is a solution for this concern. The insight to the solution comes from looking at how the airlines manage pricing. Considering the current financial state of many airlines, you might think they are not doing a good job with pricing. But if you understand and apply the premise of how seats are priced you will gather a few good nuggets. We'll discuss this more in Rule Ten.

Have a Better View of Costs

Many firms set prices based on a product or service's cost. That's a reasonable thing to do given that if you can sell above your cost you'll earn a profit. It sounds logical and it works for many. There are two issues that complicate that vision.

First, costs have nothing to do with the value those products and services create for your customers. In many cases, the financial value is much higher than costs. We'll talk more about this in Rule Four: Know Your Value. Recognize that in those cases, you are leaving money on the table and often, lots of it. Costs are an internal look at a business. Value is the external view that is much more reflective of how you can really price to increase profits.

There are a few situations where cost-plus pricing works during inflationary times. In some cases, like distribution, the cost-plus pricing model works well because the increases from manufacturers automatically flow through. Especially if every competitor employs cost-plus within a channel, then the volatility of the market flows right through to the end-customer. If the demand is still strong at the end-customer, then they should be able to absorb the up-lift in price. Some of the issues with this strategy are as follows:

- Competitors tend to be undisciplined, so there is a tendency to price low to gain market share.
- The prices will flow through as long as the demand is strong. If the demand weakens, then you could be left holding a lot of inventory that can't be moved. Your ability to predict demand relative to supply becomes critical with this strategy.
- With a cost-plus strategy, you are assuming that the manufacturer is actually increasing their pricing in a disciplined manner. If they aren't, then you have overinflated pricing that's going to your customers and that is not sustainable.

Common Tactics That Lead to Problems

Pricing is about more than setting prices. Pricing represents a strategy to increase sales volume at a profit while incorporating and communicating critical signals about the value the offering delivers to the customer. In general, most organizations fail to use pricing in such a disciplined fashion.

There are four pricing approaches that organizations still employ:

Pricing to Cover Costs: Here, you set prices based on your costs and add a reasonable margin. It makes sense to do this because if your pricing strategy is to recover costs plus a little extra, you'll always come away with a profit. Right? Not necessarily. There are two problems with Price to Cover Costs. First, your customers don't care about your costs. They care only about the value you deliver. By ignoring the value that you create for customers, cost-based pricing can keep prices lower than they should be, thus leaving money on the table and reducing profits. On the flip side, pricing to cover costs can actually keep prices higher than optimum, thus reducing sales. The second problem with cost-based pricing is that it allocates overhead and/or fixed plant costs into pricing calculations. Sounds reasonable until you consider that often those costs appear to be variable when they aren't. If you have low utilizations, your allocations are going to be high, preventing you from dropping the price to increase sales and subsequently the utilization. Again, you either forfeit profits or sales. Sometimes both.

Pricing to Gain Market Share: In this strategy, prices are set low to gain share against a competitor. Again, this sounds like a clever idea. We all learned that increasing market share leads to increases in profits. The reality is not that clear-cut. If you already enjoy high market share, it's true you're going to be more profitable. But it's more likely that you are not the market share leader. In that case, using lower prices to go after market share is risky. You can't expect to catch your competitors by surprise. Even if you do, the advantage will be temporary. The market leader will simply match your price. Lower prices eat into profits of both companies. It's a race to the bottom for the competitors while customers watch gleefully. Customers love a price war.

Pricing to Meet the Market: If you know that your costing systems inflate the true costs, maybe you use market-based pricing. Here, organizations let the market set the price. We hear about this approach a lot, and on the surface it sounds good. We know that the efficient market hypothesis has factored in every contribution to costs and prices. Here's the problem with Pricing to Meet the Market: We don't sell to markets. We sell to customers. And customers, being unique, often surprise us by behaving differently than markets predict they will. Often, they demand lower prices, and—efficient market hypothesis be damned—we often give it to them. In the end, market-based pricing is just lowering price to close a deal or to meet the price of the lowest cost competitor, which, in a global market, represents a sub-optimum pricing strategy or, in less formal terms, is just dumb.

Pricing to Close a Deal: Now we're on to something. Pricing to close a deal is what business and pricing should be all about. If we can't price to close a deal, what good is pricing, right? The process should work to provide us with a profit. Well, not really. When you price to close a deal, it provides customers with every incentive to negotiate for lower prices. These customers put salespeople through a meat grinder of price negotiations. The process, in turn, gives salespeople every incentive to respond with lower prices. It undermines their confidence in prices and leaves money on the table. We make matters worse by paying our commercial teams to do that when the incentives we provide reward them for producing gross revenue instead of profits.

The problem is that these strategies are often in place at the same company. Often, each department uses a different strategy. These approaches are not only in conflict with each other, but they also fail to effectively provide profitable sales. Instead, they can undermine revenue and profits.

Moving to a Profit-Based Approach

Profit-based pricing is a path to a more confident pricing strategy that does not leave money on the table. If you have clearly defined benefits that give you an advantage over your competitors, you should price based on the value you offer customers. In other words, a profit-based approach depends on the strength of the impact that can be demonstrated to customers.

This is a journey that takes time to implement effectively. The profit-based approach offers a road map to get there, breaking down the steps to the ultimate objective of profit-based pricing. We favor an incremental approach, rather than radical as full-speed-ahead transformation effort, a steady progression will lead to confidence in pricing that is internalized throughout your organization and resistant to the pressures that tend to erode selling backbone.

Organizations that price with confidence see the effort as a team sport. They recognize that improving their pricing capabilities requires the understanding and support of every major department and leader in the organization. It is one thing to say that your people should understand their value to customers and that your offerings, sales strategies, and pricing should be defined by this value. It is quite another to execute with this kind of commercial alignment throughout the firm.

Slow and Steady Wins the Race

If you try to move too quickly, efforts can backfire. Customers will rightly be confused and concerned. As a consequence, they will negotiate even harder or, worse, abandon you. Competitors may see your efforts to price differently as an opening to take market share. They'll start undercutting you on deals and put enormous pressure on your sales teams to react. And without the proper training and tools, your sales teams will be defenseless and frustrated by new pricing approaches that don't make any sense to them. Leaders must anticipate and manage these forces to achieve pricing leadership.

One services firm that we work with started its pricing journey well. The CEO took the lead in announcing to the world and the investment community that "rational" pricing was a priority and that the firm would be dedicating significant resources to it. The CEO established dedicated pricing departments in each major line of business. The company also created a new function that collected and analyzed costing, operations, and competitor pricing data. It put a lot of impressive intellectual effort into creating pricing models that considered value delivered to customers, not just traditional time, and materials measures. But the changes were too much for the organization to absorb quickly. It soon became clear to us that the effort was more than the organization could bite off at once.

Fortunately, the same management team saw this as well. The company took some deliberate steps. The first step was to assess what was realistic to accomplish, given existing resources and time frames. From this assessment, they learned what they were doing right and where renewed effort would be required. They further concluded that some key systems were not ready to undertake such a large-scale upgrade. Moreover, they concluded that their company lacked critical data in such areas as their own costs and competitor pricing.

Pricing Maturity Model

In the end, the company kept its long-term vision but eased up enough to allow the organization time to catch up to the vision. To keep things moving with a focus on more attainable goals, the company developed a pricing maturity model that reflected current, anticipated future capabilities, and related them to specific approaches to pricing. That process represented a reasonable set of attainable goals over time.

The maturity progression focused on improvements in three key areas. The first was continued progress on efforts to define and standardize key service lines so they could innovate to grow more tightly. The second was greater data and insight from additional analyses of costs to serve customers. A third insight was that valuable data could be gathered from failed projects, or projects that did not produce the results the client wanted.

These same projects typically exceeded their scope or budget. By analyzing what drove these shortcomings, the firm began to understand the root causes of service failures. This realization allowed the company to improve service value while focusing on controlling costs. These actions helped the company improve the capabilities of the sales organization to define, measure, and sell value, thus putting backbone in the selling process.

The leadership team determined that it could make three changes within four years. In the first year, the focus was on improving internal data, making informed assumptions about the value of the services, and getting the right people in place. While it built these critical pieces, the company tweaked its current cost-plus pricing models to reflect its steadily improving knowledge of costs to better leverage their high-value differentiators. In year two, the team set target costs and published detailed pricing guidance for the majority of the solutions. For years three and four, the company's objective was to collaborate much more closely with clients to understand value and roll out profit-based pricing models for those services where clients could see measurable evidence of value.

Results were very encouraging. By year two of the process, the value of signed contracts increased 32% and earnings jumped by $320 million. These impressive results arose from two key insights. The first insight was that it isn't necessary to achieve some elusive ideal state in pricing to see big improvements in financial performance. In fact, that's the beauty of tackling pricing. Small steps forward can produce big results.

The second insight was counterintuitive. Successful initiatives to improve price are rarely pricing-driven. This team understood that their vision of improving pricing was going to be enabled by better offering definition, cost management, sales skills, and data analysis. The firm continues to show improvements in revenues and profits. This has been possible because management is honest with itself about what the organization was capable of achieving.

The Two Levels of Pricing

Pricing occurs at two levels: strategic and tactical. The strategic level involves, first, setting pricing and offering strategies and, second, establishing the price model, price level, and metric. They also decide on approach price to value, cost-plus pricing, market-driven pricing, or a combination.

At the tactical level of pricing, managers focus on transaction prices and the rules of engagement for price negotiations. At this level it is important to make sure that customers fairly earn discounts and street prices are consistent with long-term strategic objectives. If discounting occurs, it should be for a legitimate reason, such as the guarantee for a longer contract time frame. As shown in Figure 1.1, both strategic and tactical pricing combine the activities that are at the root of pricing with confidence.

The Pricing Leadership Framework (Figure 1.1) offers three important insights. First, adjustments at the tactical level can generate incremental revenues (that drop straight to the bottom line) in a relatively brief period of time. Second, changes at the strategic level involve processes that are more involved with more effort to change. Third, change at the tactical level at some point

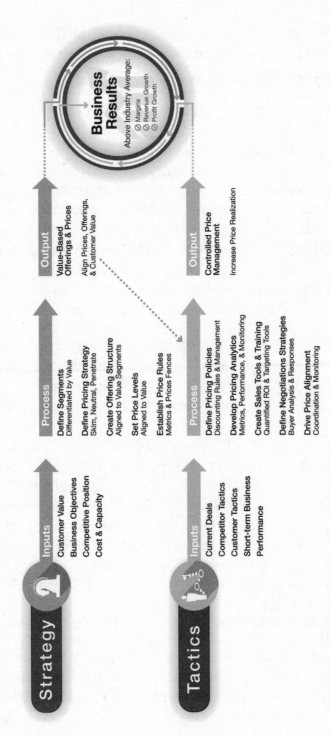

FIGURE 1.1   The Pricing Leadership Framework

needs to be supported at the strategic level (Rule Five: Strategy Sets the Direction); meaningful action is taken at the strategic level. The challenge is how to move forward at both levels by setting short-term goals that can be reached while continuously moving toward a long-term vision of pricing to value.

It is well accepted that a 1% improvement in price results in an 11% boost in net profits, according to research conducted by Mike Marn and others at McKinsey. If we go a step further and get tactical pricing processes under control to eliminate unnecessary discounts, we find that typical gains in net profit can exceed 20% profit improvement. This often causes companies to work at the tactical level and be quite satisfied with the results. For those companies that decide to work at both the strategic and tactical levels, improvements can exceed 40% in profit improvement.

Consider the case of a $3 billion semiconductor company that implemented tighter controls on discount management and deal evaluation. To ensure these controls had impact, they also implemented a globally integrated revenue and pricing plan. At the same time, the firm had been investing heavily in innovative technologies to bring truly new products to market. This combination of tactical discipline and a newly invigorated product line paid handsome dividends. Within 12 months of the roll-out, profits increased by over $400 million. The interesting part of this story is that at the time of this turnaround, this company was still in the pilot stages of transforming its pricing capabilities. Let's look at some ways of starting the process.

Criteria for a Confidence-Building Pricing Process

Key to building pricing confidence is the knowledge that it will stand up in the field with sales and customers. Improving your tactical pricing rules and processes is an essential element of that building process. Even if you don't have a formal pricing department in place, you can boost revenues by just tightening up discounting. We recommend that the pricing transformation journey starts with limiting discounts. Given the returns, getting control of transaction pricing should be a top priority.

Most companies have common complaints that include too much discounting; a lack of consistency in how discounts are awarded; and slow, unresponsive price quotations processes. The challenge with this litany of pain points is there isn't good criteria for a new process that will set them on the right path. Without agreement on what a fair price management process should look like, and the implications of inflation, companies are not able to nimbly prepare price changes.

Final Thoughts

The key to improving pricing confidence is to pick a path that the organization can follow. Rare is the organization that can quickly make the move to a value-based approach. Even capable companies face customers and competitors that are not accommodating. Start with the low-hanging fruit.

The good news is you can increase profitability just by improving your discounting controls (Rule Three: Kick the Discounting Habit). Start by refining your discounting controls and build up to become better at setting prices and defining your coordinated pricing strategy. The full evolution may take years. But at each step, you are sharpening your organization's sense of its value to its customers and driving improvements in results that will make your company more profitable, more competitive, and more confident.

There is nothing like persistent inflation to concentrate the minds of business leaders. Our hope is that as the nation's senior business leaders develop strategies for inflation, best practices in price strategy will likewise be incorporated. When pricing strategy gets the attention of senior executives, enterprises have an unprecedented opportunity to introduce long-overdue adjustments that will bring their pricing models in line with best practices and help them respond to volatility—whether it comes in the form of inflation or something else—now and in the future.

CHAPTER 2

Rule Two

An Ounce of Execution Is Better Than a Pound of Strategy

The most critical responsibility of executives is to execute. Unfortunately, corporate leaders spend more time formulating strategy and less on execution. The businesses that achieve consistent profitability are usually led by executives who, first, manage an effective price policy (the strategy) and, second, ensure that the prices set by the policy get implemented well by the sales professionals and commercial teams (the execution). They make sure that the sales teams are well prepared with the right value conversations so that customers understand the prices as fair relative to the value the customer receives.

Would you rather have better strategy or better execution? It's a question that many leaders wrestle with, although in truth we are here to tell you that no leader has to make that choice. It's a false dichotomy. You don't have to choose one or the other. Well-prepared leaders can create the conditions for deploying equally successful strategy and execution. Yet because so many leaders believe they must choose one at the expense of the other, it's useful to dispel that myth. As always, the place to start in dispelling a myth is to define terms.

Strategy is all about achieving objectives effectively. Strategy is effective when it reflects an inspired vision of the future. At the C-suite level, strategic decisions include defining such fundamental "should" questions as:

- What business should the company be in?
- What competitive advantage should the company exploit?
- What capabilities that differentiate the company and its products and services should be pursued?

Execution embraces all those decisions and activities leaders undertake in order to transform the defined strategy into profitable commercial success. Strategy execution is the implementation of a strategic plan in an effort to reach organizational goals. It comprises the daily structures, systems, and operational goals that set your team up for success.

About 90% of businesses fail to reach their strategic goals. A sobering reality is that even outstanding strategic plans fall flat without effective execution, says Harvard Business School Professor Robert Simons, who teaches the online course "Strategy Execution." His research concludes that failures of business strategy are always due to insufficient execution. "In each case, we find a business strategy that was well formulated but poorly executed," Simon says.

Our main point is that while there are certainly trade-offs between strategy and execution, there is no conflict. Norman Schwarzkopf, the general who led the coalition forces in the Gulf War, knew that leadership requires a balanced commitment to strategy and execution. "Leadership is a potent combination of strategy and character. But if you must be without one, be without strategy," Schwarzkopf said in 2012. Echoing the general, we say, "Business excellence is a potent combination of strategy and execution. But if you must be without one, be without strategy."

Keep It Simple

One reason we think strategy is over-rated is that most models of strategy are just too complicated. Business managers can't understand multidimensional models of strategy and therefore cannot do an excellent job of executing them. Companies that have inspiring strategies that everyone understands do a much better job on execution. Consider Netflix. At one point, Netflix was in the mail order business. Users ordered a movie and Netflix mailed out a DVD. When users returned the DVD, they could order another one.

In 2008, Netflix CEO Reed Hastings made a strategic decision to exit the mail order business and convert to digital distribution. The timeline for the transition was five years. This decision led to an even grander strategic vision: Netflix would eventually be in the content business. The message to the stakeholders was simple and compelling. Now the challenge for Netflix was to execute on that strategy. Executives defined the digital distribution business, created a mission statement, hired the right team, set goals and timetables, determined fees, and, most important, established the right incentives. These were the activities Netflix required to produce results within the context of the strategy. Most analysts agree the execution was near flawless. That's one reason why Netflix is the world's leading subscription streaming service today.

One factor is that the managers charged with execution—the salesforce, commercial teams, customer service—rarely have the training or authority to question the strategy. They are incented to execute the plan whether it's right or wrong, whether it works or not. The most effective solution is to keep strategic plans simple and empower managers, the people closest to the customer, to question it.

Great Execution Starts with Outcome-Centric Thinking

"It all starts with data." This is a truism that most of our clients accept when the conversation is about analytics. We also argue that it all ends with data. Which is to say, the conversation begins with objectives, which then drive the analytics needed to generate insights to help accomplish those objectives and leads to desired outcomes. Underpinning this process is an understanding of the data that is required to do the analytics (Figure 2.1).

Too many times we have seen clients spend millions of dollars on data infrastructure and tools without considering what they will use it for. Instead, they focus on data visualization under the context of building visually improved dashboards that gives them visibility into all kinds of processes. For such cases, the analytics strategy, such as it is, has the goal of bringing together as much data as possible, creating limitless views of the data, and generating novel data-driven reports.

We argue that for most businesses with real problems to solve, such capabilities are useless. The views are untethered

Outcome Based Approach

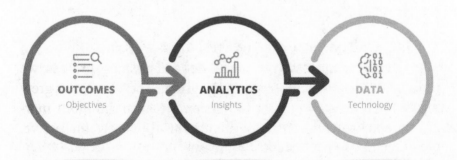

FIGURE 2.1   Outcome-Based Approach

from consequence and the porting is typically used to manipulate data to support a decision that has already been made. Analytics uses data and math to answer business questions, discover relationships, predict unknown outcomes, and automate decisions.

It's easy for businesses to misunderstand the cause and effect of analytics. They want to improve their decision-making and reduce ambiguity. That's certainly a laudable goal we support. But here's where businesses get analytics wrong. The drive to collect data must take a back seat to knowing the ultimate destination: a clear understanding of the decision or decisions they want to improve. At a minimum, this requires businesses to be able to name, describe, and model the business decisions the analytics is supposed to address.

That's challenging work, so it's understandable that the temptation is to assume that if a business accumulates enough data, filters it, puts it through an algorithm, integrates it, and displays it on a 100-inch screen visually, then the quality of decisions will improve. In fact, the ROI on such investments in analytics will be elusive. The resulting systems may generate reports in milliseconds and present the results in graphically arresting ways. But if a business hasn't defined the particular business decision or process to be improved, the more sophisticated the analytics, the more it adds to ambiguity.

It's easy to undermine analytics. In one of our projects, in response to the need to drive a well-defined business process, we developed a sophisticated reporting system. The VP of sales grew increasingly frustrated with the system because the profit margins it reported seemed to the executive insufficiently impressive. The executive ordered us to eliminate the 10% of transactions that represented the lowest margin for the business. The goal was to report more acceptable monthly profit margins. We find that analytics systems get undermined like this in all business sectors, at all levels.

Even in these times of low-cost storage and high-speed analytics at reasonable prices, we still live in a world of silos, which prevents us from truly extracting the value that sits right in front of us. We see situations play out when companies become reporting- or data-centric instead of outcome- or objective-centric and that departments start creating their own data sets for their own teams. An executive at one of the leading price optimization companies told us, "We still look at data in silos, be it marketing data, or sales data, or pricing data. We need to look at it as corporate data, so we can use it to get corporate intelligence."

Limiting undisciplined negotiation on prices is a common outcome most companies strive for. Yet, there are rampant undisciplined negotiations where deviation requests are typically rubber stamped.

Why is limiting undisciplined negotiation on prices so difficult to achieve? The answer is that most businesses don't have a pre-determined action plan for the negotiation analysis they are performing. Most companies report on "depth" of negotiation on a transaction. Depth refers to how deep of a discount a sales representative gave for a particular transaction. The deeper the discount, the more likely for a conversation between a rep and a manager. Most of the time we don't see that conversation happen because the reports are ignored. On the rare occasions where such a conversation does take place, the rep invariably reports that "the customer was getting a cheaper price with a competitor, and I had to match that price." The conversation usually ends there because the manager hasn't been trained in how to respond. The action plan with this example is not presented to change behavior. There needs to be a better assessment of competitive pricing for that negotiated product (e.g., a conversation with the product management team) as well as a program to train the sellers.

Simplify Analytics

It always amazes us to see how much time and effort clients put into "big data" analytics, but so little on insights that drive actions for business benefits. And the key to creating action from insights is to provide it at the time of need. Doing an analysis from two quarters ago is not as effective in triggering action as when the insight is given at the time of the transaction to change a behavior.

Insights can be driven off simple correlation models in Excel and pivot tables. It doesn't have to be a multi-factor regression every time. We had a SaaS client recently who had a differentiated product, and they based their pricing on 12 different variables to account for every case imaginable. The reason they called us was because customers were giving them feedback that they could not understand nor calculate their pricing. Big surprise. One of the analyses we did was a simple correlation model in Excel to see which variables were correlated to price. It turned out that they really could price based on just two of the variables. It was a drastic change, so they settled on three variables.

The point here, don't make things difficult because people will give your insights more validity if you use higher levels of math. Validity comes from insights generating an action to make the company money.

Elasticity Analysis Provides Insights

At the beginning of the pandemic, a client decided it was a suitable time to impose a significant, across-the-board price increase. In fact, it proposed a 100% price increase. The leadership asked for our endorsement of their strategy. Our instinctive impression was that the proposed price increase was risky and overreached, just as we started the pandemic lockdown.

We listened to the presentation. Their price professionals had done their homework. It was a very impressive presentation on the price increase and its expected impact on revenues and profitability. The presentation argued that the new products about to be introduced justified the price increase. As we followed along with the written presentation, we were struck by a detail in small type at the bottom of a page, almost as a footnote. The detail persuaded us that the proposed price increase was not only justifiable but could be defended as fair. We were struck by the results of the elasticity analysis. It was positive.

Price elasticity simply measures how demand changes as a result of a change in price. It is calculated by dividing the percent change in demand by the percent change in price. The relationship is usually negative. For example, when the fares for airplane travel go up, demand goes down. That's an example of negative or "normal" price elasticity. With our client, we saw a rare example of positive elasticity. That is, demand had a positive relationship to price. The analysis concluded that if the client raised price, demand would actually increase, and it did.

It was clear that their customers needed the products under consideration; price was less of a consideration than reliable supply. That insight by itself was a good justification for the price increase. Yet there was one more detail. The confidence that the price increase could be called a "fair" price. Fair is an element of value, which is partially communicated in the elasticity analysis, but it's never enough.

To decide on whether to implement a price increase, the pricing department had done an investigation of competitors. The study demonstrated that competition priced their products dramatically higher. At the same time, the market rated the competitors' products lower in quality. For these reasons, the leaders decided that a 100% price increase could not only be justified but would be perceived by customers and salespeople as "fair."

The theoretical part was well done. The client understood that even when customers secretly thought a price increase was justified, they would still complain. The execution included training of executives to make sure all the leaders agreed with the increase and to give them tools to respond to objections.

The next step in the execution was to collaborate with the account representatives for the top ten accounts. The agenda was to plan for what to do when the customers escalated their displeasure, as customers always will, up the management ladder up to, if necessary, the CEO. When the increases were presented to the test customers, we then evaluated their initial reactions and the arguments they used. We trained the salespeople to resist engaging with the customers' price complaints. Instead, we trained the salespeople to defend the price increase as fair based on the cost of providing the higher value and to do that during a global pandemic when many businesses were struggling with supply chain issues.

Through this training, the salespeople were persuaded that the senior executives were going to support the increase and expected them to do the same. What happened? The price increase stuck. There was no rampant discounting. Sure, some customers threatened to go elsewhere—and some actually did for a while—but most eventually came back and accepted the price increase.

Better Value Messages and Customer Targeting

One of the objectives of creating high-value impact messages is to identify customer triggers of value. These messages are critical when positioning a price increase. They are operational or profit-model characteristics that allow salespeople to qualify customer needs through simple questioning techniques. These triggers can be based on how a business is operated, what its central strategy is, or a combination of factors. Once these triggers of value are understood, they can be reduced to a compact list of questions that help salespeople identify high-potential prospects. The key is that the questions must be clear, direct, and result in concrete answers. We have found that salespeople welcome such tools.

We worked with one company that was providing a service to better manage printed marketing materials. The company built its business around increasing efficiency and reducing waste in the development, management, and distribution of such materials. In talking to customers about value, we found that they could reduce customer literature costs by 20 to 40% in the first 12 to 18 months of a contract. One of the qualifying questions to target customers may seem surprising: "How much dust is on your catalogs?" If printed catalogs in the storage room had a layer of dust, it was a good indication that the customer had printed too many catalogs, or their distribution wasn't professionally managed.

Once our client identified customers that overinvested in catalog pages that were literally gathering dust, it used its knowledge of customer value to present a clear, quantifiable, and relevant value proposition. Due to its efforts in researching customer value, the team was able to back up this claim with case studies and customer testimonials.

"We are able to reduce your costs by reducing obsolete inventory and by using our technologies to better match supply with your actual literature needs." Now the team had a compelling opening step to prove value to their customers. "To show you what we can do for your business, we'd like to start with an assessment of your current approach to using and managing marketing collateral. We will provide a road map for significant improvements in the costs and effectiveness of your current processes and programs."

By asking some simple questions the company began demonstrating financial impact for customers:

- "By using our service, did you see improvements in the management of your printed marketing materials?"
- "If so, what were those improvements and what was their impact?"

Now the company targeted the right customers with the right value messages and impact, and the business grew at a rate of 20% per year the next two years.

Identify the Customers You Can Serve at a Profit

Within the global view of markets, identify which customers and markets you cannot serve at a profit. If some customers are marginally profitable, but others are significantly more profitable, is your company better off serving the former, or are you better off focusing resources on the more profitable opportunities? It's a matter of defensive strategy. It's simply better for you that unprofitable customers are served by your competitors. It's one less burden for you and one more for them.

It's important to determine which doors you do or don't want your salespeople knocking on. If you don't identify these doors, salespeople will waste their time and sell to customers that don't

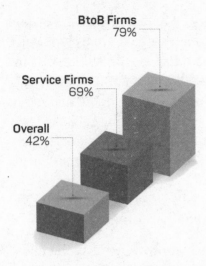

BtoB Firms
79%

Service Firms
69%

Overall
42%

FIGURE 2.2 Percent of Companies That Respond to All Customers

value your offerings. Figure 2.2 shows that unfortunately, the track record B2B companies in customer targeting and selection is not good: 79% of B2B companies are undiscriminating, responding without analysis to all customers, according to research cited by Lion Arussy in his book, *Profitable: Why Customer Strategies Fail and Ten Steps to Do Them Right* (John Wiley & Sons, 2005).

The 80/20 rule often governs this discussion. Also known as the Pareto Curve, the 80/20 rule says that, on the average, 80% of business derives from the remaining 20% of the business. As a result, we tend to focus on the big customers who drive most of the business. We let distributors manage the 20%. Is this a good strategy? Not always. Big companies are more than twice as likely to be price buyers, according to Holden Advisors research.

To better highlight the problem, cost accountants have developed what they call the "20-225" rule. Robin Cooper and Robert S. Kaplan, authors of Profit Priorities from Activity Based Costing (*Harvard Business Review*, April 15, 2000), have shown that once the cost of supporting customers is considered, only about

20% of customers are profitable. In fact, these 20% of customers account for 225% of the profits. Of course, this means that the other 80% of customers lose 125% of the profits. This principle applies equally to both private-sector and public-sector organizations.

The reality is that serving a sizable percentage of customers represents a loss for any business. The challenge, of course, is for a company to distinguish between the customers it can serve at a profit and those it cannot. It's like the time-proven adage attributed to department store mogul John Wanamaker more than a century ago: "Half the dollars I spend on advertising is wasted; the trouble is I don't know which half."

In the case of distinguishing the profitable customers from the unprofitable, the first thing to do is go for the low-hanging fruit. Start by making a list of all your customers, from the most profitable to the least. Ensure that your most profitable customers get the lion's share of resources. Then focus on the 5 or 10% of your customers who are least profitable and fire them. These are the customers getting the big discounts but who fail to give you the big volume they invariably promised. These are the high-maintenance customers who the customer service department has on speed dial because they are so demanding. These are the customers who pay late. In other words, these are the customers who cost the company to service and keep on the books.

Firing them will do three things. First, it will increase your profits even though, at first, it may cost you some sales revenue. Second, it will send the signal to salespeople and customers alike that the company has pricing standards and is willing to stand by them. Your sales and customer service people will love you for it. Finally, it will free up your selling and service resources to pursue more profitable customers, who can add profits and revenue to the firm.

Because they are desperate for business, most managers will resist terminating customers. We don't like to do it either. The goal, of course, is to convert unprofitable customers into profitable ones. Before making a unilateral decision, we recommend that you have a candid conversation with the customers. Tell them why the relationship is not sustainable in its present form and let them know you are prepared to end the relationship. Some percentage of those bottom customers will understand and offer to keep doing business with you on renegotiated terms.

How Effective Are Your Price Discounts?

The essence of strategy is the efficient allocation of scarce resources so as to achieve maximum return. In other words, if you are going to do something as a manager, whether it is spending time, money, or both, for the sake of the company, you should have a basic understanding of what that expenditure is going to return in terms of added profits and added sales.

Consider the things you routinely do. For example, you attend meetings to discuss new products or more efficient operations—two important activities designed to increase sales and profits. If you are going to give a price discount, don't you want to be sure that the discount drives added revenue and profits for the company?

Limiting undisciplined discounting during negotiations is a common outcome most companies strive for. Yet, there is rampant discounting, and deviation requests are typically rubber stamped.

More than likely this is because most companies don't have a pre-determined action plan for the discount analysis they are performing. Most companies report on "depth" of negotiation on a transaction. Depth refers to how deep of a discount a seller gave for a particular transaction. The deeper the discount, the more likely there is a need for a conversation between seller and a manager. Most of the time we don't see that conversation happen because the reports are ignored; if we do, then the answer from the seller is almost always, "the customer was getting a cheaper price with a competitor, and we matched that price." Then the manager walks away.

Here is what a true outcome-centric analytic process should look like for limiting undisciplined negotiation. First, determine if it's a behavior issue, a broken process issue, or if it is market driven. This process is required because the root cause determines your course of action. So, we would have three outcomes under negotiation and not just one.

For behavior issues, we recommend doing the analysis of seller negotiations by products and by customers (Figure 2.3) to see if they negotiate in whole percentages (e.g., 5%, 10%, 15%, etc.).

If we find sellers here, then the pre-determining action would be training and then monitoring for change. For broken

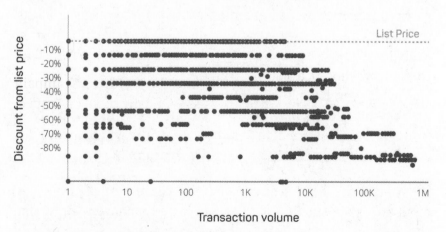

Signs of Undisciplined Discounting

Price per transaction distribution

FIGURE 2.3 Signs of Undisciplined Discounting

process issues, such as discount approval rates north of 50%, which should trigger an investigation to understand the validity of the process in place, maybe we need to change the threshold for escalation, or maybe the manager needs more training.

The market-driven scenario is the most difficult root cause to attribute. How do we determine if it is truly a competitive scenario? We have seen clients manage this in two ways. One, by having detailed reason codes that you can search on in CRM to determine how often and on which products this customer uses this as their reason. Two, we have also seen clients measure how often competitive price comes up in their daily reason codes and see if there is a deviation from the rolling average for a similar peer group segment. If there is a large deviation, then you know a competitor is making price moves on a particular product.

As you can see from the example of limiting undisciplined negotiations, analytics doesn't always have to have a data scientist involved to have business benefit. Your actions from your insights have already driven the value.

Control Discounting with Rules of Engagement

After your review of the outcomes from the discounting analysis, the commercial team needs to decide when it is clearly a mistake to give discounts. It may be with small customers. It may be with customers who purchase your high-value products and services and where you have little competition. It may be in certain geographic markets. It may be with salespeople who haven't been through value training. The team must identify where to give discounts and where to stop giving price discounts.

We call these rules of engagement. Simple rules of engagement are established to let salespeople and managers know that you are beginning to limit price discounts. At the same time, you let it be known that you are willing to let some business go. If you have done a decent job defining the rules of engagement, it shouldn't cost you valuable business. By that, we mean you hopefully have identified where it is wrong to be giving customer discounts. If they decide to leave, it is going to be good for your business. If a competitor takes them, it is great for you and the competitor suffers the deterioration of margins.

The trick to rules of engagement is to start with something easy. We have seen companies with all sorts of data infrastructure, from completely fragmented to a single source of truth and everything in between. Our guidance is that there is no data perfection. Start with customer usage and transaction data. Once insights are gleaned, decide what the right "budget" is for discounts per region per customer segment, etc. The rule of engagement should be that every customer that wants a discount must earn it.

Put teeth into the new rules of engagement, or you're wasting your time. Sales managers will just keep internally negotiating for more. One company we know reviews seller's discount performance on a yearly basis and fires their most extreme discounters. This kind of "rank-and-yank" strategy has other costs, but it definitely sends a message about what the organization values.

We have never seen strategy outperform execution. On the other hand, execution supported by a leadership team aligned on price policy will consistently outperform the limitations of strategy, structure, capital allocation, and even market conditions.

CHAPTER 3

Rule Three

Kick the Discounting Habit

Discounting is a habit entrenched in many organizations. While discounting is a tool that pricers deploy, habitual discounting sub-optimizes customer relationships and leaves money on the table. In many cases, discounting turns into an addiction. Discounts are simple and deliver short-term KPIs. Once an organization falls into the discounting addiction, the battle is lost even before the negotiation begins. The best way to dislodge any deep-rooted attitude is to replace it with another. Backbone signals to the entire sales team that a new confidence and exciting new tools are in place to kick the discounting habit.

The dangers of rash discounting show up in even the most basic analytics: customer plots, win loss reviews, and customer profitability analysis. It becomes cultural in organizations, and sellers rely on it as their crutch for closing business. If you have a culture of discounting, your customers know it and will not trust any proposal you offer. This is what led us to Rule Three: Kick the Discounting Habit.

Successful commercial teams invest the time to understand how they create value for customers and know how to engage in value conversations. The best companies know they have to display just a little arrogance about the value they offer in order to send an important signal to potential buyers. That signal is: We are confident in the value we provide and, therefore, the prices we charge. Moreover, kicking the discounting habit creates space to present other areas of differentiation, such as product, presentation, logistics support, customer service, etc.

This attitude replaces the knee-jerk reaction of dropping price with the powerful conversation-starter: "Can we share the results of how we helped another company solve a business problem similar to yours?" This question replaces the "tell" that many sales teams signal to customers and prospects that there are discounts to be had. All the customer has to do is push for more value, a lower price, or both. How you react sends them a signal of your "seriousness" and confidence in your value.

Procurement people are trained, incented, and managed to drive cost savings for their company. They focus on getting discounts. Smart salespeople prepare ahead of time for this conversation with Give-Gets vetted by the commercial team. That little bit of arrogance acts to level the playing field between the buyer and seller and for sellers, the courage to demand a fair payback for value.

Kicking the Discounting Habit

How many times have you felt the need to discount deals to meet your quarter or year-end sales objectives? We have yet to meet a client who could honestly say "never" to the discounting. When you have responsibilities to run a business, the pressure to keep the revenue flowing, to meet payroll, and to keep employees productive is tremendous. That pressure is sometimes alleviated when markets are growing and customers are plentiful. But when industries slow down, as they inevitably do, the pressure to discount goes up exponentially.

Let us be clear, the problem is not discounting. Sometimes lowering price is the optimum response. It's the habit of discounting—the unthinking and throw-caution-to-the-wind desperation—that's so destructive. It's the addiction to discounting and planning every sale to include one. The difficulty with discounting, as with all addictions, is that it is difficult to stop. Organizations get used to discounting. They defend it as "industry practice." Our clients tell us, "We have no choice but to discount because our competitors are discounting." In fact, the competitors just look like they are unreasonable because they have the same addiction. By the way, the competitors describe you to their customers the same way.

A good place to start in kicking the discounting habit is to calculate what the habit is costing the organization in profitability and lost opportunities. This is not an easy calculation to share because it requires a number of awkward conversations that have the goal of the organization acknowledging it has a bad habit. Denial is a powerful force. What's required is a disciplined and fearless pricing team that is good at tracking the discounting. If you want to even think about challenging a habit, a good first step is to invoke the price/volume plot described in Rule One.

Cycles of Desperation

Take a look at the situation from the point of view of the salesforce. When salespeople get their objectives or quotas for the year, they base their ability to deliver results on a number of assumptions of their own. Assumptions such as having the right product mix, delivering products on time, and getting a feel for what competitors do. This is where the wheels begin to fall off the wagon. Nothing ever happens as projected. Interest rates go up. Currency exchange becomes unfavorable. Product delivery is interrupted. Competitors drop prices (imagine that). Customers get more price sensitive. When things don't go as expected, it leads to what we call cycles of desperation.

Suppose the salespeople have been trained to negotiate well. Or they have a limit to how much they drop price. In either case, the results are the same. Salespeople do the best they can to hold the line. Do they get rewarded for that? Nope. What happens is that at the end of the period—month, quarter, or year—if the organization is short of the projections, managers get off their collective behinds and go out to do what is necessary to close the gap. That means closing business with customers, whatever it takes. There's an old business adage that says that if the only tool you have is a hammer, all problems look like nails. So it is with managers who need to make the numbers. They have a problem, and the only tool they have is price. Hence the reflexive discount.

The White Horse Syndrome

Managers today want to be regarded as heroes, saving the day, avoiding awkward questions. Instead what they usually do is drop prices. And far from solving their problems, they undermine the organization's value proposition. We call this the "White Horse Syndrome" in honor of television shows in which a complicated problem of long duration is resolved when a hero such as the Lone Ranger rides into town in a cloud of dust on a white horse to save the day. Then, as quickly as he arrives, the hero departs, saving everyone the unpleasant task of asking awkward questions such as, "How did we get into this mess in the first place?"

One manager refused to play this no-win game until the division president got desperate. It was a business downturn, and the division president's bonus was at risk if the division did not deliver on goals. The executive's reaction was predictable. He authorized an end-of-month discount to distributors who would buy forward. The results in the first month were great: The company made its numbers that month and the division president enjoyed his bonus.

The next month turned out different, of course. In order to take advantage of the generous discount, customers had placed the order to cover the needs of the current month so there was no order this month. What did the executive do in response? Yes, he ordered another discount for buyers to fill up the pipeline. This strategy is unsustainable, and we know that what is unsustainable will have to stop. Did the company make its numbers? No. Remember, they were in a business downturn. The company needed to adjust its expectations, not manipulate pricing to generate groundless numbers.

The company stopped its discounting lunacy in the third month and decided to face the music. In the last week of the third month, the distributors were clearly holding their orders, waiting for another price cut. When the additional price cuts didn't materialize, customers started calling, asking when the discounts would be coming. When they heard that there were no more discounts, they started placing their orders as they had done in the past.

Using price as the primary competitive weapon in most markets doesn't buy any additional business; it just gets customers to focus more on price and less on value. The executive missed his numbers and had to forfeit his bonus. But worse, the company lost hundreds of thousands of dollars in profits by offering discounts they didn't have to.

White Horse Syndrome Effect on Sales Force

How about the effect of the White Horse Syndrome on the sales force? The salespeople quickly learn that if the managers are going to focus on price, they should, too. They stop focusing on value. They worry less about being good negotiators. When a customer asks for a lower price, they either give it to them or say they have to check with their manager. In either case, the customer knows they have won. Salespeople begin to have less regard for what is in the long-term interests of the company. They stop listening to the value rhetoric coming out of senior executives' mouths.

To make matters worse, the firms that buy into the White Horse Syndrome begin to develop systems that formalize the dysfunctional process. Forms and policies are created to dictate who can control price. Whole departments spring up to support the process. Price exception requests accumulate. Everyone learns how to play the game. Smart salespeople learn how to be the internal squeaky wheel that demands and obtains the lower price for their customers. Uncontrollable discounting becomes part of the corporate culture, embedded in the corporate DNA, unexamined and unexaminable. Confidence in any pricing strategy goes out the window.

Then the gross rationalization starts. Executives mistake the difficult conditions they have created for a state of affairs they cannot control. The mantra becomes, "Boy, it's a brutal industry we're in." Pessimism becomes a badge of honor. Talk about value is dismissed as irrelevant. "Hah! Value selling will never work in our industry. It's too tough here," they say. Fortunately, nothing could be further from the truth.

Here's an example of how this works. We were recently collaborating with a senior executive interested in kicking the discounting habit in his business unit, a division important to the large conglomerate. We helped the executive build price/volume plots for several product lines. He and his team calculated the plots, considered the outliers, and figured out which customers they could expect the sales teams to control. Did he get pushback? Sure, he got a lot of resistance. But with only a very few exceptions, he used his authority to create the confidence his sales teams needed. The result? Dramatic increases in both units sold and prices paid. In part, his work made his division the star of the conglomerate.

Never in a Vacuum

Discounting never occurs in a vacuum. Companies and managers develop systems and processes that allow discounting to flourish. Discounting occurs despite vigorous attempts to control it. Many companies have implemented systems that place barriers on salespeople who want to offer discounts. Managers do that because they think it limits the discounting. The company institutes a deal exception process to review requests for deeper discounts These processes get more cumbersome and more people in the chain of command review deals. The president of the business unit must sign off on discounting requests. Soon that becomes 80% of their workload.

It's this discounting mindset that gives customers the entry point for obtaining lower prices that are often not necessary to close the sale. We don't blame customers for negotiating for discounts. We blame the discounting habit. We've seen discounting justified in every conceivable way. Some companies justify it by customer. These companies start off by giving discounts only to their largest customers. These are the big customers, perhaps the marquee opportunities in the industry, and they order lots of products and services. Perhaps the volume of business they transact legitimizes the discount. But invariably the companies succumb to discount creep, the expansion of a project or mission beyond its original goals, often after initial successes. Then the midsized and smaller accounts start getting discounts, too.

Many companies justify discounting by product. In these cases, discounts are offered only for commodity products with intense competition. Again, discount creep kicks in. Pretty soon, the company's newer technology, innovative high-value offerings start getting discounted, too. Sure, there are some justifications, such as the ability to get the low-value commodity products put on the purchase order as well. But the results are the same. Companies end up leaving money on the table in the negotiating process.

We worked with a SaaS company that provides data to enable its customers to target consumers for precise marketing campaigns. The company was founded by two engineers who developed an innovative algorithm-based data solution. Like most engineer founders, their focus was not on pricing but on data manipulation and their delivery platform. The founders spent all their energy growing the company and partnering with each customer to increase usage metrics. After hitting a milestone of $100 million in revenue, the founders realized that their pricing strategy wasn't keeping up with innovation in technical areas. They asked us to make recommendations about how they could optimize pricing.

We did an assessment and immediately discovered something we didn't expect. The company was exceptionally good at resisting demands for discounts from new customers. In fact, the company was really good at onboarding new customers willing to pay the undiscounted list price. Then we looked at historical pricing data. Now the situation became problematic. We were able to demonstrate that the longer the company served a particular customer, the more likely the customer would get a discount.

This behavior might be justified if the discounting generated more volume per customer. To evaluate this hypothesis, we overlaid the discounting behavior against the volume per customer. Guess what we found. Change in price had no significant impact on volume. The sales team was just giving price away to keep their best customers happy.

We also found that their market was not very elastic based on how their customers used their product. Customers were either going to use the SaaS product or they weren't. Rarely did a high or low price determine how much of the product they were going to use. Basically, the volume they were getting was consistent while the pricing fluctuated. We chatted with their customers and determined that they can in fact increase price based on the value they were providing and not lose any volume based on how the customers used their solution. The company put a stop to such discounting and saw increases in revenue and profits.

Desperation Pricing During Inflation Won't Work

We are in the worst inflationary period in four decades. Every expectation is that inflation will be with us for quite some time. Based on the calls we are getting; we understand that many of our clients are concerned about operating in inflationary times. Here's our first piece of advice: You are not alone. No one has experience operating in inflationary times. Moreover, there's nothing you can do about general inflation. It's bigger than any individual corporation. It's bigger than any individual nation. It's truly a global dynamic.

Companies with a culture of discounting will really struggle to implement effective price increases. These increases to cover increased costs are vital. All customers must take the increase. If not, the company will suffer from Dumbbell Pricing, that is, high prices for some customers and low prices for others. This will cause your most loyal customers to lose trust in you and drive your overall base to poker-playing behaviors.

Our second piece of advice about inflation: realize that you can't "price" (i.e., discount) your way out of inflation. Why? We'll talk about that in Rule Five: Strategy Sets Direction. All discounting will do is attract the price-sensitive customers who you probably won't want to deal with because such buyers tend to be unprofitable. And that's the best scenario. The worst scenario is one that happened recently with one of our clients.

We were engaged by a professional services company, which confronted both an increase in costs (inflation) and a slowdown in demand. What did the company do? It started discounting to make up for the decline in demand. Of course the strategy failed to address the business problem. After we reviewed the situation, we understood two things. First, we saw that the company was discounting without benefit. In other words, the discounting did not generate the uptick in demand it anticipated. Second, the impetus for the discounting was coming not from the sales team closest to the customers but from the increasingly desperate senior leaders of the organization. The problem, we understood, was worse than just discounting. The company had actually started a price war with its competitors, leading a race to the bottom where demand was as elusive as profits and revenue. The solution was to develop some Selling Backbone (Rule Nine: Build Your Selling Backbone to Increase Profits).

The third piece of advice: stop and think about what you are doing. When in the midst of a crisis, its leaders may be sorely tempted to do something, anything. But rather than reacting to the problem, first stop and consider what may be the actual root cause. Think through the problems of discounting and look for a better way. In some situations a company must hunker down, cut costs, and possibly survive during the problem years. That's how we and many of our clients got through the pandemic and the last recession.

Inflation imposes a unique set of challenges. The worst response is to do nothing for too long and then decide that the only way to survive is a drastic price increase. The results are usually predictable. The departure of your best customers and a dramatic decline in profitability. Even if the discounting succeeds in onboarding new customers, they tend to be price buyers. These customers tend to fill up your business with special requests, complaints, returns, and other demands that overload your service teams. Meanwhile, the service teams have less attention to your best, most loyal customers, causing some of them to jump ship for better customer service. It's difficult to convert price buyers into the kind of loyal, profitable customers that companies depend on.

What to do in times of inflation? Raise prices surgically as soon as you see your costs rising. Don't make the mistake of annoying your customers with incremental price increases. Raise prices and justify the increase with an apology, a justification, and a commitment to use the increase to find ways to continue to provide better products and services. Most customers have done the same thing with their customers, so they will understand. And while you're adjusting for inflation, take a hard look at the price buyers who may have crept into the customer mix. Most of these price buyers are probably unprofitable for the company. Fire them, and let your competitors have the honor of losing money on them.

None of This Is Easy

We understand that as readers consider the lessons of this book and our associated advice, they may think, "It's easy for you to say." It isn't. Just like you, we have a business to run, customers to service, payroll to meet. None of the advice we give is predicated on the idea that any of this is going to be easy.

The second objection we often hear is, "You don't know our industry." The truth is, both sets of objections are raised by people who resist change. Now, change isn't easy. We tend to focus our energies on clients who see the need for change and want a hand in understanding what change is needed and how to make the transition as smooth as possible. We never tell clients that the change will be easy. As for those who resist change, our first task is education. We want to communicate the benefits that might derive from a change in how the organization confronts issues about pricing, competition, and discounting. We've learned that, irrespective of product or service or location around the world, the habit of discounting can be brought under control if the firm's leadership sets their mind to it.

CHAPTER 4

Rule Four

Know Your Value

Value is the foundation of all business activity. Know it, own it, and prosper. The goal of Rule Four is to connect you in a fundamental way with the measurable value your customers have determined your offerings contribute to their go-to-market effort. If you can do that, pricing suddenly becomes more precise and transparent. If pricing is akin to playing poker, knowing your value eliminates the customer's capacity to bluff. It's as if you can see your opponent's hidden cards.

Why Value?

For what job is your customer hiring your product or service?

The late Harvard Business School professor Clayton Christensen used this question to get to the heart of what a customer wants a product or service to do. Customers "hire" your products to do a certain job that is to their advantage. That advantage, as determined by the customer, represents a clear channel to the question of how to measure the value that your offering delivers to your customers.

This book focuses on business-to-business (B2B) pricing. Business buying is more complicated than selling to consumers, where prices are more or less non-negotiable. It's unlikely that a consumer will ask the checkout clerk at Wal-Mart for a discount on a quart of milk. Understanding customer value is the core of B2B pricing. Businesses buy because they often convert what they buy into something they sell to other businesses. While the volumes can vary by a lot or a little, the impact within the operations of a customer's business can be dramatic. Understanding value is also important because B2B customers expect to negotiate. Sellers cannot defend price without understanding and having confidence in value.

The Power of Value and Use in Inflationary Markets

Basing pricing on value is the method of setting a price to earn a portion of the differentiated worth of its product for a particular customer when compared to its competitor. Customers buy a product or service to procure something of value in excess of what they have to pay for the product or service. Understanding that value helps you set a fair price for the product or service in question. Creating a culture that encourages salespeople to understand and believe in that value inspires them to be more confident in the sales and negotiating process. Creating alignment with a value culture is the critical success factor for senior leaders of any organization.

Value is king, even in an inflationary market. Think about being a customer and seeing a price increase on a product that you love to use. If that price is still below the value that you measure by using that product, then the increase is warranted. A price increase on a product where you are taking only a share of the value for your customers should be one of the first things you do in an inflationary market.

Conversely, anytime the customer concludes you are no longer priced fairly based on that value, it becomes more of a difficult conversation. The customer starts considering alternatives. In this situation, the most important questions to ask are, what are competitors doing, how sticky is this customer, how profitable is this customer, and what's my ability to change prices in the future?

We recommend pricing based of the value you deliver to your customer. The important note here is to set the price to invite the customer to capture value while ensuring you as the supplier capture a share too.

Adopting a Value Mindset

Understanding value comes from a business skill every member of your commercial team needs to cultivate: listening to customers without an agenda. Customers will happily give you the information commercial teams need to build critical insights about value, but not if they feel the team members have an agenda besides listening.

Such a listening tour does not have to be a big, complex research project. The most powerful insights usually result from asking direct open-ended questions and listening. In this information gathering mode, sales teams can be vital sources of wisdom. In fact, everyone who has contact with the customer at any stage of the sales and support cycles can engage with a value discovery mindset. Every opportunity for customer intelligence will have a beneficial impact for your own firm.

There is one question that we do not recommend you ask your customers. And that is, "What do you think of our prices?" Asking directly about your prices is an invitation for customers to posture. Every customer asked will agree that your prices are too high. Is that surprising? Your customers have every incentive to try to get you to believe this. Worse, this approach derails the conversation from its purpose.

The best questions center on their requirements and key problems that need to be solved, the benefits provided by your offerings, and how the two interrelate. The key is to understand your value to your customers and then use this information to support the fairness of your pricing. By showing that you understand your value and demonstrating that your prices are reasonable given that value, you change the discussion. It is no longer just about price; rather, it's about value and then price.

We recently did value research on a product that was sold to large financial institutions. We started with primary market research, which focused on getting an understanding of the benefit that customers would get from using the product. Only after we determined the value proposition did we assess customers' responses to a limited range of price increases. The benefit, or the value in this case, far exceeded the price that the research showed customers would accept. As a result, our client was able to increase prices, which were accepted without complaint by customers. It's a good example of how leveraging Rule Four resulted in increased revenues and profits.

Listening to the occupants of the C-suite requires a different approach than listening to procurement managers. For lower-level stakeholders, it's completely appropriate for listening teams to ask a series of discovery questions. Not so for senior executives. For senior executives, lead with insights, not questions. Your job at this point is to deliver value to executives while you glean insights from them. It's not for them to educate you on their business. Research and preparation are key. If you get time with any member of the leadership team, you should know their business and pain points and enter into a conversation which delivers insights into the opportunities, risks, and solutions they might not have considered.

Why Talk to Customers About Value?

Your customers are the greatest source of information on value and value based on their use of the product. This can be different for different companies, and value should not be one-size-fits-all. To investigate the details of how value is perceived, we recommend asking two questions:

- "What is driving needs and attitudes?"
- "What are the implications (for both the supplier and the customer) of addressing those drivers?"

By answering these two questions, we can answer an even more fundamental one:

- "Where, precisely, do we provide value in our customers' businesses?"

Without answers to these questions, companies are adrift. Businesses want to focus their resources on the best opportunities to provide financial value to their customers. And they especially want to concentrate on cultivating those areas where the business value can be differentiated from competitors. Gaining insights in these areas can have a profound impact on any business. It positions businesses to create even more valuable offerings, target the best customers for those offerings, and to empower their sales organization to sell value and defend prices.

For pricing confidence, it is critical to understand some fundamental aspects about customers, their businesses, and what it is they value. These insights achieve a number of important outcomes. The insights pave the way for better segmentation and targeting and the creation of offerings that are deemed by the customers to have value. The insights also serve as the foundation for well-defined price-value trade-offs (see Chapter 8, Build

Your Give-Gets Muscle). Superior value positioning and better pricing are additional benefits of these insights. Figure 4.1 summarizes the power of understanding your value to your customer.

The progression of questions and objectives in Figure 4.1 underscores an unexpected point: the more you appreciate the value you deliver to your customers, the greater confidence the commercial team will have in the price. In this case, knowledge protects and can increase profits. But it gets even better than that.

FIGURE 4.1 The Power of Understanding Customer Value

The knowledge cascades as part of a progression that sharpens your marketing strategy, product management, and sales techniques. It is with these activities that we create and frame our value to our customers. When firms apply their understanding of customer value in this way, positioning prices as fair relative to the value provided is quite simple.

Customers Want to Talk About Value

For the skeptics. The objection most frequently raised when we recommend asking customers about how they define value and how a supplier contributes usually takes this form:

> *Why would our customers share this kind of information?*
> *They'd be crazy to talk to us about how they make money*
> *and how our offerings help them make more of it. Won't*
> *they be afraid we would use that information against*
> *them? Won't they see this as a ruse to get them to give us*
> *the justification to raise our prices?*

Our experience is that customers, as a rule, do not react like this to good faith questions from suppliers. Of course, customers must have some basis for trust. A long-standing partnership usually provides a foundation for trust. Commercial teams, in turn, must demonstrate that they are sincere in collecting the information for their mutual benefit. In other words, if the perception is that the information will help customers operate more efficiently, then customers may well appreciate the conversation. In practice, most customers are eager to talk about their businesses, their goals, and their efforts to be successful. Their motivation for doing so is simple. The more their suppliers understand their business issues, the better able those suppliers will be to craft solutions that are relevant and valuable.

It takes good listening and probing skills to gather this information. It also requires shifting your point of view from an internal perspective (a focus on the value you believe you deliver) to an outside-in perspective (the performance, benefits, and value as perceived by your customers). Only the latter view counts, as the customer determines value.

There is one final consideration. The analysis must be done in the context of your specific competitors. Customers always consider solutions in the context of competitors. No business operates in a vacuum. When customers think about suppliers, it's usually in the framework of how one performs relative to competitors.

One of our clients produces heavy equipment. Its value challenge was that there was little differentiation between its products versus a key competitor. As much as 80% of the equipment components were common to the competition. Given this commonality, the industry was racked by cutthroat price negotiating and discounting. Our job was to establish a basis for the client to defend its pricing. We started by interviewing the client's customers to determine if there were points of differentiation we could leverage. The initial plan was to conduct 30 customer interviews in each of nine segments.

Over the course of just the first six interviews, we gained enough information to show our client that its products provided demonstrably more value than the competition. When our client's most important customers talked about what they appreciated about our client's business model, they had a common response: The value of their dealer network. This network was almost twice as large as the next largest supplier. The customers saw over and over again how the scale of the dealer network reduced downtime, decreased operating costs, and kept revenue-producing assets in the field.

If a customer, for example, needed a critical part and its local dealer didn't have any in inventory, the part could be obtained very quickly from another dealer in the network. With just a handful of interviews, we learned that customers perceived an incremental value of 15 to 20% buying from our client products relative to buying a similar product from the competition. Our client used that information to focus its marketing efforts and defend its prices.

How Does the Customer Obtain Financial Value from the Use of the Offering?

When talking to customers the goal is to drive the discussion to a dollar sign. Dig deep for financial value, otherwise any talk about value to the customer is just noise (Figure 4.2).

We were collaborating with a company that offered a wireless infrastructure solution. During their initial internal discussions, the IT and services people focused exclusively on the technology of the product. Their comments focused on the technology, process, design, and integration services that they delivered to their

FIGURE 4.2   Connecting Features to Benefits to Value

customers. These elements are important, but they are not what the customers wanted to talk about.

Customers were more concerned about geographical coverage of services, uptime, and reliability of the platform. With coaching, the supplier team learned to demonstrate how each of the features cited by technical staff focused and aligned with the benefits that the customers wanted and what subsequent financial results were realized.

The financial connection comes from a process we call *drilling down* during internal and external interviews. This is the tactic of probing to uncover the details underneath the customer's first answer, which is often superficial. The drill down generates critical value insights because it moves well beyond the cursory or top of mind answers that most customer research yields.

We were working for a software company interviewing the CEO of a systems integrator. When we asked the executive why reliable messaging was so important, the executive answered that half of the company's technical support budget would be saved if the company had reliable messaging. The bottom line is that we were able to determine that if they had reliable messaging in their software tools, the firm would save $300 million in technical support and software development expenses. Getting to *why* represents the best opportunity to provide a quantifiable ROI for selling the right offering.

The information-gathering effort required curiosity and a willingness to ask simple open-ended questions and then listen. This last point may be the most difficult because listening without judgment or preconception is not easy. This process is not difficult for those firms that want to do a better job of understanding their customers. The constraint is that many managers find themselves bogged down in day-to-day activities to accomplish these tasks with customers in mind.

Customer Interviewing

It is important to prepare well-thought questions to conduct interviews. There are three distinct steps to think about: preparation, execution, and integrating results.

The technical term for the actual interview is exploratory depth research. It is exploratory in that it uses your insights to develop hypotheses about how your customers value your products and services. Through multiple interviews, the hypotheses are confirmed or revised. It requires an in-depth interviewing approach in that probing techniques go beyond superficial answers. Ideally, it surfaces real points of pain your customers have and what they value when looking for a solution. The goal is to find out how product or service features reduce costs or increase prices and sales. These are the real value drivers of a business.

When doing depth research with a client's customers, we find:

1. The real drivers of customer value are somewhat different than the selling firm expected.
2. The current solutions are more valuable than estimated by the supplier.
3. Customers are pleased that someone is finally asking them about their business in a meaningful way.
4. There are opportunities to provide much more value than suppliers currently offer.

To transform the information into real insights you need to summarize the key points, important customer quotes, and financial implications from each interview. The important thing is to keep track of your insights on customer value drivers, possible value positioning, competitive value positioning, pricing, and possible product or service enhancements. This library is powerful for making value real for sellers and should be kept up-to-date to help create case studies to support your value over time.

We helped a supplier of business forms conduct this process in the banking industry. At the time, this supplier offered 150 individual services on an ad hoc basis to its customers. Many of these services were provided on request without charge. Based on the customer interviews, our client discovered that a majority of the banks identified a specific bundle of these services as especially valuable. The client was further amazed that the bundle of services cut across a number of banking segments that were

Problem: Rationalize - 150 Individual Services

Simple Agenda - Understand

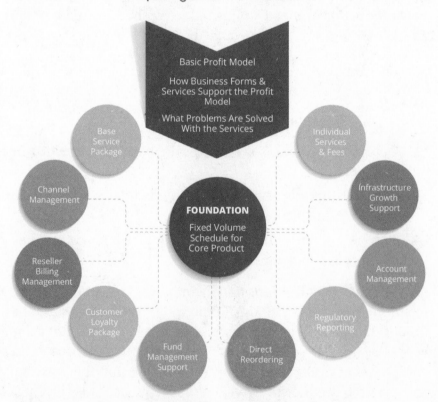

FIGURE 4.3 Using Customer Value to Simplify Offerings

otherwise ignored in their models. In fact, they found that they could dramatically simplify their service offering and start charging for that service bundle. The client was leaving money on the table by not recognizing the value of these services.

As a result of these insights, the client rationalized the bundle into 10 segmented service packages, each priced accordingly. The offerings also included a bare-bones basic service package (see Figure 4.3). When the services were rolled out, the supplier reversed a 5% per year decline in profitability and began growing at 5% per year in a declining industry. Much of this success can be attributed to the fact that the connection between the customer's business model and their high-value needs was easy for the sales force to implement. The sales team asked each prospect three questions about their business and how they planned to grow. With the answers to these questions, the seller was able to quickly select the best offering for the customer and position it with concrete value statements.

Simple and Consumable

Over the years, we have interviewed the salespeople, and they admit that they just didn't trust the black box value calculations. We listened closely and concluded that the best value analysis must be simple and consumable for salespeople. Our guide is to make it simple enough that it can be displayed on the back of a napkin.

A few years ago, we were asked to do a value study for a large medical device company. They had a device that was disposable and would replace a popular non-disposable device in use around the world. The advantage our client offered, unlike the incumbent device, which needed extensive cleaning before re-use, was that it was a disposable device and didn't require cleaning. A problem of the incumbent device was that if it wasn't cleaned properly, the possibility of cross-patient contamination was present.

The medical device company engaged several of the larger consulting firms to do extensive value work that resulted in detailed, complex spreadsheets to determine the pricing of the disposable device. It was all detailed down to the tenth of a cent. When we saw the spreadsheet, we were impressed by the sophistication of the calculations. At the same the calculations measured the wrong thing, and the sales team did not want to use it.

The medical device company had targeted large teaching hospitals as prime targets but were struggling to gain adoption. To help increase the velocity of adoption, we identified the underlying problem. The focus was on the wrong target customers. It came down to the value advantage perceived by the customers. Large teaching hospitals tended to have excellent programs to train people on how to clean the devices. The likelihood of cross-contamination of patients was extremely low and therefore not a concern to the hospital team. Adoption was low because the company focused on the wrong market cohort.

We suggested that smaller hospitals, which didn't have the highly effective training programs, were likely to be more logical adopters. We further suggested that hospitals that serviced immunosuppressed patients were even higher in their likelihood of purchase, as cross-contamination would be viewed as a critical issue. These hospitals would be expected to see value in disposable devices that would eliminate the possibility of cross-contamination. The value for this product was in risk mitigation.

The trick to understanding value is to try to put that understanding into a series of back-of-napkin calculations that help salespeople and customers see how the features of your products and services create value for your customers and their products. Our change of heart proclaims this takeaway: you are better off being approximately right than precisely wrong.

To summarize, link how your product and service features create benefits for customers and the benefits of that value in specific financial terms. Make sure to connect the dots. We see a lot of companies that stop at the benefits, expecting customers to make the final linkage to financial value.

Capabilities Needed for a Value Focused Organization

Pricing clarity comes into focus when commercial teams connect with the measurable value offerings contribute to the go-to-market effort of the customers. Every successful business must offer a product or service that differentiates itself from the competition. The most successful businesses are intensely customer-focused, in that feature sets and improvements are based on the customers' wants and needs. Another critical way that businesses express differentiation is through pricing. It follows that customer-focused pricing becomes a strategic response to the customer's perceived value of a product or service. Businesses that offer unique or highly customized features or services that are aligned with the expressed desires of their customers are simply better positioned to defend their prices.

Figure 4.4 presents a capability matrix which is needed to support all pricing activities. As you can see, no one function is at a level required to be consistently effective for value-based pricing.

One risk with parsing these needed capabilities across different departments is the likelihood for unhealthy and conflicting prioritization of activities within functions. This means the pricing team would spend most of its time negotiating with functional leaders to gather the right information rather than executing on the end goals. This wastes time that you don't have in a volatile market.

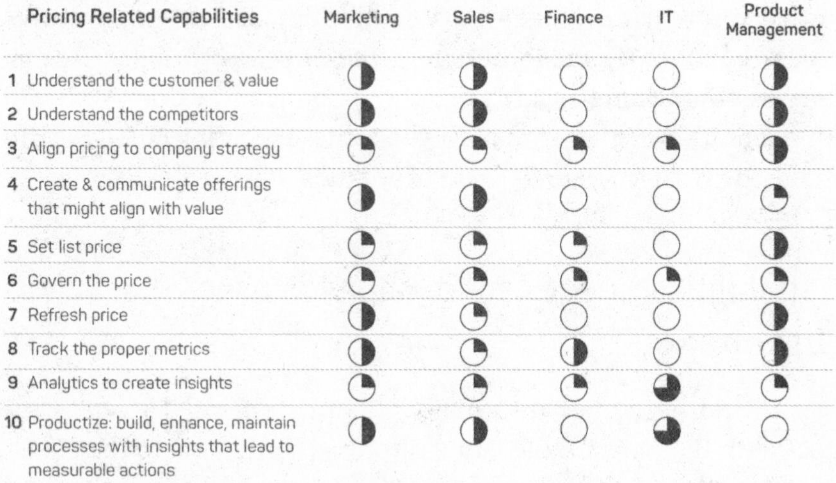

Pricing Related Capabilities	Marketing	Sales	Finance	IT	Product Management
1 Understand the customer & value	◑	◑	○	○	◑
2 Understand the competitors	◑	◑	○	○	◑
3 Align pricing to company strategy	◔	◔	◔	◔	◑
4 Create & communicate offerings that might align with value	◑	◑	○	○	◔
5 Set list price	◔	◔	◔	○	◑
6 Govern the price	◔	◔	◔	◔	◔
7 Refresh price	◑	◔	○	○	◑
8 Track the proper metrics	◑	◔	◑	○	◑
9 Analytics to create insights	◔	◔	◔	◕	◔
10 Productize: build, enhance, maintain processes with insights that lead to measurable actions	◑	◑	○	◕	○

FIGURE 4.4   Pricing Related Capabilities Matrix

Another structural design flaw we see are smaller pricing teams spread through different functions across different regions. These teams tend to be specialized for local and department needs. Silos are an unfortunate effect of such localization. No one person is charged with supervising the company's interest holistically. Deal profitability is parochial, and sellers focus only on specific product lines by region.

To develop effective pricing—to achieve pricing with confidence—it's important for companies to develop all 10 capabilities identified in Figure 4.4. For that reason, we most often recommend that the pricing team be centralized. The only caveat here is that for a conglomerate with disparate product offerings and/or markets served by the individual companies, it often makes sense for pricing responsibilities to be dispersed.

Because pricing is a strategic lever for organizations, most have found that the pricing reporting structure should be into the C-suite. The pricing team needs to have influence and ownership.

What's more, the pricing team needs to be seen throughout the organization as having influence. Reporting into the C-suite provides the pricing team with the gravitas to be successful in achieving the end goals. Having said this, any pricing organization must be horizontal in its approach. Meaning, it needs to collaborate like a team sport with multiple functions to achieve those end goals. A pricing director of a large global electronics manufacturer told us that pricers need to be "multi-lingual," that is, they are able to speak finance, IT, marketing, operations, and, of course, sales.

The Behavioral—Social—Dimensions of Pricing

This book focuses on the tactical and strategic dimensions of pricing. Yet we would be remiss if we didn't address the behavioral dimensions of pricing because, stated as directly as possible, pricing is a group decision. Pricing in an enterprise context incorporates the group decision dynamics of pricing committees, pricing departments, and ad hoc pricing teams. Furthermore, the agendas of executives aligned with the interests of various functional departments (finance, marketing, accounting, engineering, sales, production, etc.), each with adjunct responsibilities for price-setting, must be included in the mix, underscoring the essentiality of group dynamics around pricing. As Gerald Smith, a business professor and chair of the Marketing Department at Boston College in the Carroll School of Management, noted, "With so many voices involved in price-setting, there is an important imperative: to understand 'how pricing gets done around here—*socially*.'"

The pricing department, group, or team should be at the center of price management activities harnessing the data diversity and decision diversity resident in corporate functional departments. As Smith noted in his influential book 2021 book *Getting Price*

Right: The Behavioral Economics of Profitable Pricing (Columbia Business School Publishing), resolving the social parameters of pricing requires managers to ask some fundamental questions about group dynamics:

- Who engages in pricing?
- Who is influential?
- What biases are present?

All these questions and biases determine how a team goes about price-setting. Biases are often driven by the "functional nations" from which managers have been trained, each with a different professional culture, different language, different key performance indicators (KPIs), and different ways of approaching pricing. "Where the managers identify—Finance, Accounting, Marketing, Sales, Production, Engineering, and Pricing—help determine the values, priorities, and prerogatives that determine pricing," Smith said.

"Still, these diverse organizational departments offer valuable data and skills that are vital to price-setting. For most firms, according to Smith, the key to achieving profitable pricing is to focus on two cognitive pillars that should undergird the pricing decision process: *data diversity* and *decision diversity* across the price-relevant domains of the organization. This means tapping continuously into the influence perspectives from the four cardinal pricing orientations (Figure 4.5) and their champions within the organization," he said.

"Doing so exploits the price-relevant skills—both soft and hard—of each of these different corporate functional nations, while debiasing the price-setting process with a constant awareness of the strengths and weaknesses of each—a system of checks and balances if you will that leverages decision diversity," Smith said.

FIGURE 4.5   The Four Cardinal Pricing Orientations

Companies exhibiting sound pricing discipline use their pricing departments or groups to achieve a *balanced pricing orientation*. For example, Adobe reframed its pricing strategy in 2012 using subscription pricing, a major shift in pricing strategy. Quite apart from the administrative effort, what really impressed us was the coordinated effort across the finance, accounting, engineering, marketing, and sales functions that resulted in such an effective, coordinated shift in pricing strategy. Professor Smith describes a corporate boardroom converted into a new pricing "war room" with its walls posted with the most up-to-the-minute pricing analyses, updated continuously with feedback from each of the functional price-relevant disciplines. The transition to the new pricing strategy took five years from initial launch with constant refining, adjusting, and listening to customers to arrive at an emergent pricing strategy.

CHAPTER 5

Rule Five

Strategy Sets the Direction

The right price strategy uses price effectively in all conditions to preserve both revenue and profitability. The right strategy ensures you have accounted for your value, competition, market growth and customer adoption, and objections. Finally, it makes sure you execute by engaging a committed and knowledgeable salesforce.

Setting an organization's price strategy, difficult in the best of times, is complicated by the distortions of actual inflation and, more, the expectations of inflation. Chapter 5 demonstrates the fundamental importance of getting the price strategy on sound footing to defend the tactical and operational pricing decisions up and down the organization. It requires nothing less than the concerted efforts of everyone in the organization to marshal all the levers of pricing to ensure that resources are deployed in the most efficient and effective manner possible.

Price Strategy and Inflation

The right price strategy adapts to a high inflation environment. Nobel Prize–winning economist Joseph Stiglitz sees prices increases as a "healthy balancing of supply and demand." We believe that increases in demand are desirable for a business but failure to adjust pricing effectively to take advantage of those increases can leave a lot of money on the table.

Pricing can't "solve" the economic problems that we are all now facing. What a price strategy can do is mitigate some of the damage in terms of lost profits and revenue rising inflation imposes on businesses. The good news is that in times of inflation, consumers and business partners expect to see price increases. Inflation watchers note that demand, especially for manufactured goods and professional services, remains strong. This demand remains resistant to price increases. While you may not be able to price your way out of a recession, you can price your way out of inflationary times, especially when consumers expect you to increase prices and, at the same time, are willing to purchase more to manage their own spikes in demand.

The smartest pricing leaders also acknowledge that inflation and supply chain disruptions further require them to be initiative-driven in their price strategy evolution.

This kind of proactivity requires companies to be vigilant about runaway discounting. We are talking about indiscriminately applying price discounts to meet short-term sales objectives. Discounting simply trains customers to hold off placing their orders in anticipation of even deeper discounts. But there's a bigger problem than leaving money on the table. Rather than selling your products and services because customers derive value from them, you end up selling them just to meet your numbers. It's never sustainable to exchange short-term opportunism for long-term customer development. You may get a high from the adrenalin rush of the end-of-quarter madness, but you end up leaving so much money on the table, you might get asked to leave the game.

It's a game that almost all businesses play. Every year, leaders make sales projections for the business to meet. These projections get reported down the chain of command, commercial teams get their marching orders, and everyone waits for the results to be reported up the chain of command. If it turns out that the company has hit its projections, satisfaction abounds. It's a sign that management understands the market and is in control of the business. When the company outperforms the projections it is seen as evidence of particularly talented managers. No one asks why the particularly talented managers set the targets too low. This is a reactionary process that undermines both perceptions of value and subsequent profits. Being more strategic with your pricing helps firms make better decisions that protect and grow profits

Inflation and Supply Chain

Inflation and supply chain disruptions are linked. Supply chains are fragile processes that rely on business stability to work efficiently. The shock of the COVID-19 pandemic sparked a cycle of instability in the global economy that is unprecedented. Closed borders and disruptions in supply cascaded down the global supply chain. When supply chains are disrupted, businesses everywhere feel the pain. In extreme cases, businesses are forced to shutter plants and lay off employees.

Global supply chain disruptions are nothing new, but the COVID-19 pandemic compounded by inflation woes created unprecedented disruptions. Consider the microprocessor chip shortage. Millions of products now rely on tiny computers on a chip. These microchips power a wide range of products that we don't necessarily think of as "smart." But a typical automobile today uses more than 1,000 microchips. Electronics have gone from representing just 18% of a car's cost in the year 2000 to over 45% of its cost two decades later and is projected to be 45% by 2030, according to *The Economist*.

In retrospect, it's clear how the global chip shortage developed. First, demand was already outstripping supply by March 2020, when the pandemic forced many manufacturing plants to shut down while closed ports backed up container ships for months and increased transportation costs by orders of magnitude. Companies watched helplessly as their goods languished on container ships stranded in the Suez Canal or stuck at the ports of Los Angeles and Long Beach, California.

Re-opening plants is difficult; replacing those laid off workers in a shrinking labor pool is even more challenging. Businesses are increasing wages to lure back workers to re-open plants. The need for wage parity increases pressure to raise wages for existing workers. The result is inevitable: a continuing cycle of worker shortages and higher prices. Inflation causes labor costs to soar, of course. But the labor market we're experiencing is not a typical hiring boom. There's every reason to believe that even when inflation is tamed, labor costs will refuse to stabilize.

The pandemic has forever shredded the power relationship between employers and employees. Remote work has permanently changed the way people think about earning a living, with the emphasis placed more on the "living" than the "earning." Other workers who jumped into the freelance or gig economy will not soon give up the flexibility and control that comes from working for themselves. Employers who make the mistake of forcing workers back to a full-time office settings will learn that their most productive workers would rather quit.

With all of this turbulence, here are a few things to think about:

1. **Understand your market.** Make sure you have up-to-date insights into what's really happening in your market. We'll talk about this more in Rule Seven, but for now the point is to develop the business intelligence of the overall market conditions, competitors, and how inflation shocks are likely

to change the behavior of all stakeholders. We recently witnessed a situation in which a strong and dominant competitor entered one of our client's markets that had been protected from competitive pressure. Panicked, the client told us it had no choice but to react to this intrusion. We counseled a bit of patience and analysis. Careful consideration demonstrated that the competitor suffered from two deficits. First, the product it offered was perceived as a lower value alternative. Second, the competitor had a questionable approach to distribution. The analysis led to further protecting both the supply and distribution chains, which dramatically enhanced our client's competitive position. We'll talk about this more in Rule Ten (Deploy Three Practices to Increase Profits).

2. **Understand your customers.** You and your customer may have the same worries. There's power in that. If you are worrying about inflation, you might be surprised to learn that most of your customers are worried about supply chain issues. That gives you an understanding of how to position your price increases as being not only fair but also reflecting costs necessary to stabilize your supply chain. Customers see a benefit in dependable suppliers. This gives you an opportunity to respond to their real concerns and strengthen your relationship by addressing those concerns.

3. **Get more dynamic with price setting.** Look deeply at current discounting practices to get control of them. That usually means systematizing pricing. Inflation obliges most companies to establish new guidelines even as they accelerate the frequency of price changes. What worked for the stable economic environment we enjoyed for decades is upended by the dynamics of inflation and supply chain challenges. Companies that were used to re-pricing annually or even quarterly now find it imperative to re-price monthly or even weekly.

4. **Fire unprofitable customers.** We talked about unprofitable customers and the 20/225 Rule in Chapter Two. In times

of inflation where profits can erode more quickly than normal, businesses cannot afford unprofitable customers. Seek out the unprofitable customers and let them go. A little analysis reveals who these customers are. These are the customers that hammer you on terms and conditions. These are the customers who ask for partial truck deliveries. These are customers who are constantly on the phone with requests for more service even as they stretch 30-day payment terms to 120 days. The first step is to tell them you cannot continue to serve them on present terms unless they change their behavior. And here, you have to be explicit on the behaviors you expect. We saw this dynamic play out with a number of our clients. For instance, one of our clients had a long-term and mostly frustrating experience with a large supply chain distribution company. With a little training from us, the lead sales representative asked for a meeting with the president of the distribution company and announced that the client would have to terminate the relationship because it was simply unprofitable to continue the relationship. The salesperson articulated the client company's concerns and what it would take for the partnership to be mutually workable. The president of the distribution company at first dismissed the threat. But as the client pulled back from the partnership, the company understood the value it was receiving from the client, changed its behavior, and converted to a customer the client could serve as a profit. Note that occasionally a threat to fire a client must be enforced. But in our experience, more often than not, a credible threat is enough.

5. **Raise prices.** Of course you need to raise prices; do it fast but don't do it often. Make it part of a planned and periodic exercise of reviewing cost changes and passing them on to your customers. Don't forget surcharges. Surcharges are another pricing variable to consider. Customers usually accept surcharges that are justified by external conditions. In the early

days of the COVID-19 pandemic, many firms imposed Personal Protective Equipment (PPE) surcharges. Customers are familiar with the surge pricing of Uber and Lyft, as well as the rush hour surcharges on highway tolls. Be transparent about what you are doing. Position them as being fair given the circumstances. But be very careful of initiating surcharges if the satisfaction of your loyal customers is at risk. You may be better served to just increase prices.

6. **Think longer term.** Make "reliability of supply" a feature that becomes part of your selling, negotiating, and contracting process. It is one of the "Give-Gets" that customers hate at first but come to appreciate when they see that they have a dependable supplier.

7. **Consider changes in price metrics.** Switch to a price metric that helps mitigate market risks for the customer and you. An example of this is a switch from subscription pricing (static) to a usage-based pricing (dynamic). This gives the power to the customer to "control" their costs during a volatile market.

The nature of strategy in good times and bad, during times of growth or decline, recession, or inflation, is that it must adapt to accommodate the evolving nature of customers, competitors, and markets. Adept managers are continually assessing their business environment to assess not only the strategic approach of the firm but also how that approach needs to change in the evolving environment, what those changes are, and the cadence of the changes.

The very idea of a price strategy makes even the most capable managers nervous. One of our clients put the objection succinctly. "Given the dynamics of today's business environment, how is it possible to settle on a specific price strategy without limiting our ability to respond to what's happening in our markets? Markets move fast, customer needs change, and our competitors certainly aren't sitting still." Believe us, in those conditions, strategy is even more critical. The trick, as we have argued, is to keep the strategy simple.

Choosing the Right Price Strategy

There are five primary drivers in choosing the right price strategy:

1. The value of your offering relative to the competition: As we pointed out earlier, your price strategy is defined by how you set price levels relative to your and your competitor's value.

2. An understanding of where the offering is in the life cycle: This is critical because market-level price elasticity changes with each phase of the life cycle. As a result, the best price strategy for one phase is often disastrous for another.

3. Industry economics: Knowledge of the overall health of your industry (is utilization increasing or decreasing? what about margins?) and your cost structure is essential. Industries with high fixed costs need to look at price strategy differently than industries with high variable costs. Cost structure will also affect how competitors play the pricing game.

4. Competitive dynamics: Unless you include competitors' likelihood of responding to your price strategy, you are missing a critical element. An analysis of the likelihood that they will accommodate or disrupt your strategy helps define how conservative or aggressive you can be in your approach.

5. Value relative to the competition and position in product life cycle serves to define the first cut for considering your price strategy options. Depending on your market, your final choice is best reconciled with other key influencers such as cost position relative to the competition, how competitors play the competitive game, and industry economic factors such as forward capacity.

Let's look at how these factors combine with the three basic price strategies to enable the price strategy decision.

The Three Basic Price Strategies

Skim Price. An essential precondition for skim pricing is an offering that customers believe is clearly differentiated from the competition. Prices are set high relative to mainstream competitors.

Neutral Price. Companies that use neutral price strategies typically do so because they want the basis of competition for customer business to be something other than price. Prices are set close to the competition with the intention of reducing the impact of price competition. This is especially critical when entering and during the mature phase of the life cycle.

Penetration Price. Companies use penetration price strategies precisely because they want price to be the primary driver of the purchase decision. Penetration pricing works when it can be used to establish a dominant market position.

Choosing an Inflation-Driven Price Strategy

Selecting a price strategy is a high-stakes decision. Selecting a price strategy to respond to the challenges of inflation is even more fraught. So, how should commercial teams respond? Unsophisticated price leaders tend to select one of three shortsighted options. They can disappoint their customers by raising prices; disappoint their investors by cutting margins; or disappoint each and every one of their stakeholders by cutting corners in order to reduce costs. Faced with three equally unattractive alternatives, most commercial teams and most managers ultimately end up raising their prices.

Modern times are different than the 1980s, the last time inflation rates were as high as they are today. Businesses and the customers they serve enjoy a level of information access and price transparency that would have boggled the minds of their predecessors when Ronald Reagan was president. Businesses today have real-time market visibility and the nimbleness to exploit changing conditions. Customers, in turn, have much better data and tools to combat information asymmetries. Modern analytics ensure that businesses and their customers are generally negotiating on a more transparent playing field.

"Inflation [today] is a different story," says Oded Koenigsberg, professor of marketing and deputy dean at London Business School. "Managers now enjoy a level of market visibility and agility that their predecessors could have hardly imagined even one generation ago. Managers have much better data and more sophisticated tools to analyze and turn this data into a useful information to support decisions."

It's an ideal time, Koenigsberg says, for commercial teams to treat inflation as a strategic opportunity rather than a tactical challenge, and to choose from a better set of options. In his article "Pricing Strategy: Three Strategic Options to Deal with Inflation," (*Harvard Business Review,* January 18, 2022), he offers three alternative models:

- **Recalibrate and Clean Up the Portfolio.** One option is for companies to bundle or unbundle existing products, either to create new value propositions or to expose customers to lower price points for the disaggregated goods and services they want to buy.

- **Reposition the Brand.** The basic idea underpinning this option is that at any given time, most products and services are either overpriced or underpriced relative to the value they deliver. Repositioning the brand often surfaces price misalignments. Further, persistent inflation offers commercial teams an opportunity to correct these misalignments in their product positioning.

- **Replace the Price Model.** This is not as radical as it sounds. The success of subscriptions and SaaS models have required many organizations to alter new price metrics and adopt new price models. The opportunity to replace your prices instead of raising them brings many benefits, especially in conditions of persistent inflation.

Choose wisely, and improved pricing performance becomes an engine of organic growth that drives both revenue and profits. Make the wrong decision, and you can start a price war that sucks profits out of the entire industry. "Instead of worrying about how much more to charge their customers, [businesses] should devote their resources to figuring out how and why they should be charging them," Koenigsberg says.

Pricing Through the Product Life Cycle

Most products have a finite life cycle. As markets move through their phases of growth and adoption, price strategies have to change, too. Throughout that life cycle there are four distinct stages. The introductory phase is marked by slow sales growth as customers consider the benefits of the new offering. During growth, customers begin to adopt the offering in increasing numbers and the entrance of new competitors helps speed adoption. During this stage, sales volumes can grow at a breathtaking rate. As products achieve adoption by most potential customers, they enter maturity. During this phase, overall market growth slows and begins to level off. Finally, in the decline phase, sales volumes drop off as customers move on to other more up-to-date products and technologies.

Let's start with the concept of market elasticity. Elastic markets are quite responsive to changes in price. Inelastic markets are not. The concept helps pricers understand when price increases are likely to generate more revenue.

Overall market response to price (elasticity) is not the same in each stage of the life cycle. The most important thing to understand is that markets are only elastic (very responsive) during one phase: growth. As Figure 5.1 shows, the growth stage is unique in that the rate of growth is high. During this phase, customer adoption accelerates as innovative technologies start to gain broader acceptance. New competitors, seeing the opportunity, also jump in. Ironically, greater competition actually serves to increase the size of the market as more conservative customers perceive that an innovative technology is a safe bet and becomes even more widely available.

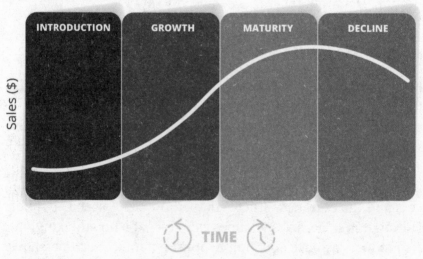

FIGURE 5.1 Stages in the Product Life Cycle

Increasing customer adoption and the increased visibility brought by fresh players in the market often combine to accelerate growth. Let's see why this is important and what causes it.

Demand in BTB markets is derived from some downstream market. This means that demand for products won't be responsive to price changes; instead, they will be responsive to how the demand in the downstream market (the customers' demands) changes. As an example, General Electric sells engines to Boeing. Boeing makes and sells twenty-four 777 widebody aircraft per year. Despite any price change or strategy that might be considered, Boeing is only going to buy 48 GE-90 engines. Demand for the engines is derived by demand for Boeing aircraft. This makes it, by definition, inelastic.

The second reason comes down to customer behavior. Some customers will change suppliers often. They don't change their volumes, something that elasticity research tries to capture. They change their suppliers, often due to price. We call that cross-elasticity of demand. If we measure cross-elasticity of demand, we can determine a market's responsiveness to our changes in price, but it is unlikely that the volumes will change. That's because demand is derived. This means that the elasticity will not bring more opportunity for volume. Finally, you need to include competitive behavior in the mix. This is the most essential element of the mix. Even if a market is elastic (see Figure 5.2), when a competitor matches your price decrease, they negate any market effect. If your market is inelastic, as most markets are, you've just burned through profits playing a game that you can't win. Sometimes we see clients struggling in inflationary markets drop prices to maintain volumes. All they have done in this situation is erode profitability and potentially shortened this phase of the life cycle.

Let's summarize how this should impact your decision on price strategy.

FIGURE 5.2   Revenue Impact of Price Changes in Different Market Conditions

Remember the only stage of the life cycle when markets are elastic is during growth. As Figure 5.2 shows, during all other phases of the product life cycle, decreasing prices will lead to long-run decreases in revenue. You may get a short high from a price cut as customers switch their business to you, but the benefits are short-lived. Competitors will simply match your prices.

Introductory Markets

The pressure to cut prices can be intense. When rolling out an innovative product or service, marketers are focused on identifying and selling to innovators and early adopters. These are customers that actively seek out new and innovative offerings before others do. Importantly, these customers are desirable because they become references for other customers, and they provide critical input that translates into market success later in the life cycle.

Given these two significant benefits, companies are often tempted to buy early business with low prices. This temptation is not necessary because customer motivations run the gamut from the logical (exploiting the latest technologies to get ahead of the competition) to the emotional (a desire to simply be the first to use an innovation). The decision to be an early adopter is also driven by a desire to advance the company's brand as an innovator operating on the forefront of its industry. Regardless of the specific motivation, early adopters are more interested in putting innovation to work than they are in price.

In his groundbreaking work Diffusion of Innovations, Everett Rogers estimated that innovators and early adopters make up 16% of those that adopt a technology. Given the limited pool of customers and their relative lack of price sensitivity, the best approach at the introductory phase of the life cycle is to pursue the skim pricing strategy. Such a strategy has significant benefits. A high initial price sets the reference for future generations of customers and revisions of the product. Also, a skimming strategy at introduction can actually improve adoption, as early customers will use price as a proxy for value. Discounting prematurely will actually undermine customer perception of value

There are two major challenges at the introduction phase of a life cycle. The first is selecting the right customers. These are customers who are more likely to accept the risk associated with a new innovation to gain a competitive advantage. If salespeople target the wrong customers, chances are they will expect a lower price for unproven innovations. Here, the price isn't wrong; the customer is. The second is in proving the value of the innovation. Companies that successfully gain adoption of their innovations do a lot of work to show their value to would-be customers. Without addressing value, the customer will focus on price to decide whether the opportunity to determine the value of an innovation is worth the price and associated costs. Intel and Apple are expert innovators. They consistently introduce their newest technology products with a skim price strategy.

Growth Markets

During the growth phase of the life cycle, the number of customers increases dramatically. In addition, many of these customers are inexperienced and will need additional services and support. Existing customers typically begin to expand their usage to peripheral parts of the offering. With these predictable forces, it makes sense to create bundles of service and support for inexperienced customers. Innovation-driven companies also respond to the increasingly sophisticated needs of their early customers with complementary product and service offerings. They evolve their offerings to meet the differing needs of both high- and low-value segments.

Since an innovative technology is still unique during the growth phase, as well as bundled services, does a skim-price strategy make sense? Not always. Here's the complication. A skim-price strategy may retard market growth or open lower price markets to competitors just as growth begins to accelerate. Sticking with a skim-price strategy too long gives these competitors a chance to enter the market with competitive technologies at lower prices. Remember that markets in the growth phase are elastic. This means that lower prices will increase demand and revenues. The key question is how to manage this. Simply lowering prices on your high-value offerings to meet the new competition may help with market share, but it will quickly erode profits in high-end segments. The solution? Be the first to break for the bottom with an option for a low-priced stripped-down offering to flank the competitor's high-value offering.

Intel deployed great strategy against AMD. Using its technological lead, Intel would skim price major new products and then drop prices significantly after the volume from early adopters showed signs of leveling off. Doing so not only increased demand but it limited AMD's ability to make sufficient margins as it responded with comparable technology. And once customers had chosen Intel microprocessors, they more often purchased additional chip sets based on Intel-provided reference designs. AMD wasn't able to break this cycle until they leapfrogged Intel's technology with their 64-bit processor. With these products, AMD dramatically increased profits and saw their market share rise to historic levels only to see them drop when Intel introduced similar processors.

Mature Markets

As a market moves into maturity, overall demand levels off and the benefit of using low prices to grow the whole industry disappears. In fact, penetration pricing is poison if you are competing in a mature market. That's because penetration pricing reduces revenue while causing profits to decline dramatically. At the same time, penetration pricing increases the likelihood of a price war as competitors will quickly match your price cuts to recover lost market share.

The best response here is to skim price for high margins at the top of the market and use a neutral price strategy for mainstream and low-end market segments. Given the need to play the pricing game at multiple levels, it's in mature markets where product and pricing managers really earn their keep. The key to making multiple strategies work is a set of offerings that enable you to be successful at all levels of the market.

In addition to manufacturing a range of high-performance, heavy-duty engines for trucks and buses, Caterpillar also offers remanufactured engines for price-sensitive customers. The company actively promotes this low-flanking offering and explains why customers might want to consider it. Customers are told that Caterpillar remanufactured parts carry a "same as new" warranty to assure worry-free ownership. Price-sensitive customers benefit from remanufactured products that cost 20 to 60% less than new products. The company benefits by having a lower-priced flanking offering for customers who resist the prices of new products. These customers remain Caterpillar customers by not defecting to the competition and may be in a position to pay higher prices for new products in the future.

There is one exception to this rule. If you are in the enviable position of being a cost leader, then all bets are off. Cost leadership has substantial and unique rewards that lead to different decisions around price strategy. Often, cost leaders enter markets not by taking on the leaders but by serving the most price-sensitive customers first. For them, penetration pricing is the strategy of choice. This approach is typically sustainable through the growth and early maturity phases of the product life cycle. As the market moves deeper into maturity, even cost leaders need to consider adding enhanced offerings and higher-end products to reap profits from niche segments that begin to appear.

Failure to understand this transition cost Dell Computer its market leadership position in 2006. In response to the threat of a newly revitalized Hewlett-Packard, Dell aggressively dropped prices to win market share. The result? Profits dropped 51% from the prior year. Commenting on their problems in a 2006 *New York Times* interview, Michael Dell and Kevin Rollins noted, "We cut prices too aggressively in a number of markets to win market share. We didn't do a good job of it at all." An increase in PC sales of 6% translated into an operating profit decline of 48%.

Declining Markets

In declining markets, diminishing demand is sustained by customers that have a strong preference for a particular technology. This preference is typically strong enough to make declining markets price insensitive.

To understand how this works, let's look at the market for a technology that many people think is dead, but surprisingly is doing quite well: vacuum tubes. These forerunners of today's integrated circuits were once common, powering every radio, television, and computer. Today, vacuum tubes are still popular among audio enthusiasts and musicians who value the warm sound qualities they are thought to deliver. These loyal customers are willing to pay for that performance. A typical price for vacuum tubes is $10 to $20. By contrast, an integrated circuit that performs the exact same functions with greater control and reliability costs pennies.

By focusing on these integrated concepts—market growth, relative value, derived demand, and price elasticity—you can arrive at the right strategy to produce healthy revenues and profits. Figure 5.3 illustrates what strategies are called for in distinct phases of the life cycle.

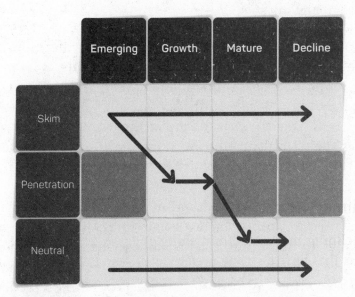

FIGURE 5.3   Avoid the "Danger Zones" by Changing Price Strategy Throughout the Life Cycle

Price Strategy for Capital-Intensive Businesses

For companies with investments in plant and equipment, consider overall industry capacity and capacity utilization when selecting price strategy. In times of excess capacity, it makes sense to adjust prices downward only to the extent that the price cut helps utilize plant capacity. Capacity share and market share tend to equalize over time. Attempts to increase share during times of excess capacity through the use of a penetration price strategy can be easily matched and negated by the competition.

Conversely, as capacity begins to become scarce, it makes sense to start bringing overall price levels up. If not, the company is vulnerable to filling capacity with low-priced business. The potential damage will be worse if smart competitors start shedding their most price-sensitive customers with the intention of foisting them on you. The end result will be a sharp decline in your company's profits.

In the final stage of the business, when the industry is operating at or near capacity, the safe decision is to pursue a skimming strategy. There is one caveat. Always treat loyal customers fairly. While in theory you may be able to extract more profit from them at the top of the cycle, they will resent having their loyalty betrayed. Long-term customer relationships are valuable. To the extent customers consider your company as a partner, they will resist taking advantage when your company is at the bottom of the cycle. While this will mean forgone profits during good times, it will also mean more stable profits during slow times when the business of loyal customers is more meaningful. There is a trick to this that we'll talk about in Rule Ten (Deploy Three Practices to Increase Profits).

The Competitive Landscape and Price Strategy Options

Price strategy must be measured against what the competitors are currently doing or are capable of doing. There are two principal issues that pricing managers need to consider. First, what is the firm's cost position relative to the competition? Second, given the different options for an emerging price strategy, how is the competition likely to respond?

When looking at potential competitive responses, there are some obvious strategies to avoid. Penetration pricing against a low-cost leader is a nonstarter. The same is true in relying heavily on skim pricing against competition that has a win-at-all-costs, lose-no-deal-on-price mentality. We'll talk more about playing the competitive game in the discussion of Rule Seven (Understand Your Market). If you are uncertain about how competitors will respond, here's a helpful hint to avoid destructive price competition. When facing a volatile competitor, a neutral price strategy is always the safest. To support your strategy, it always pays to be able to keep competitors worried that you are prepared to adopt a penetration strategy to defend your market position. This threat reduces the likelihood that they will adopt a penetration strategy against you.

Be Prepared to Change Your Strategy

It's not really that tough to pick a price strategy. The challenge comes in knowing when the market changes to act quickly with a strategy change. So what are some signs that conditions require a change in price strategy? Here are a few to keep an eye on:

Unit sales volume growth slows down: This, along with a change in customer price response, is the primary indicator of a transition from one phase of the life cycle to the next. When entering the growth phase of the market, if you grow but not as fast as the competition, it may be time to lower prices. When moving from growth to maturity, growth starts coming increasingly at the expense of the competition. When this happens, it's time to deploy multiple strategies, especially neutral prices.

Discounts fail to drive incremental volume: Look at your graphs of price discounting versus gross sales growth. When one line starts heading up (discounting) and the other starts heading down (sales growth), this is a signal that it's time to start thinking about changing your strategy.

Competitors introduce new offerings: Time to check your value positioning. Have you gone from being a leader to being a laggard? If so, you need to move away from skim-price strategies. At the same time, be mindful of Rule Six (Innovate for Growth).

Lower-cost competitors enter the market: Are you providing an umbrella for them? Will they come after your high-value customers? If so, you need to move to protect your flanks with a penetration priced offering.

Competitors start missing their numbers: There is nothing more dangerous than a desperate competitor. Time to try to take the focus off price.

What About During Inflation?

Remember, product lifecycles are a function of changes in demand and customer adoption over time. At a market level, the demand does follow the phases that we outlined, but what happens to these phases during inflationary times? If you are able to pass the cost along knowing demand is there, then no changes are needed in any of these phases. The most common question we get from clients is "what if competitors don't also raise prices?"

Let's first look at reasons the competitors might not raise prices. First, they may be more averse to the risk of driving customers away. Second, they may just be slow to respond to cost pressures. Both are fairly common reasons. In either case, focus on what you can control. Our suggestion is to raise prices in line with your increased costs and hope the competitors come to understand the situation and then raise their prices as well.

The third reason is tricky. Here the competitor decides that now is the time to adopt a penetration strategy to pick up market share. Doing that in a growth market makes sense. Doing that in a mature market can lead to a devastating price war if you respond. In this situation, the reality is that in the short-term, the competitor will succeed in taking market share. Assuming that the competitor has a cost structure similar to yours, you can assume they will bleed profit dollars. But, if anyone has a cost advantage, then they will likely come out ahead in the long-term by using this low-price strategy to gain share and still maintain profitability. The key here is to understand your competitors and take as much unneeded cost out of your system as possible so you have the flexibility to choose the right pricing strategy.

What do you do if a competitor decides to take market share during inflation or otherwise? The best approach is to develop a model that identifies the different scenarios of how a competitor might respond. Part of that modeling should be your revenue and profit implications for different scenarios. If you lower your price and the competitor lowers it again, you will quickly see that you may be better served to let the competitor take the price-sensitive customers; you may very well have been losing money on those customers anyway. We did this modeling for a medical device manufacturer that was catching up to the innovation of two primary competitors in the mature phase of the life cycle. The modeling showed that any penetration price strategy was going to lead to the lowest profits and a neutral strategy with a high-value product would limit the price competition and protect profits. The introduced product quickly gained 30% of the market with good profits.

Making Salespeople Champions of Price Strategy

Within the first 10 minutes of a pricing training session, a senior salesperson from a national bank stood up and asked, "We are compensated on revenue. How is anything you teach us going to make us more money?" It was a great question. We replied honestly: "It isn't." Revenue plans conflict with pricing for profit objectives. After the training, we suggested better aligning sales compensation with profit. Though the leaders taking the training (measured on profit) wanted very strongly to improve margins, they failed to act on our advice. Within six months, this large national bank failed. If salespeople are compensated to achieve sales volume, they will drop price and even go below discount floors to close a deal.

How do we support our salespeople, through compensation plans, tools, and messaging, to become the champions of the organization's price strategy? How do we get their buy-in to do so? These are the crucial questions that every company must address.

Many companies don't see the obstacles to creating sales champions that drive growth in both revenue and profits. There are four common reasons that cause salespeople to advocate for more discounts for customers, rather than profit for the company:

1. Sales incentives are misaligned with the company's financial goals.
2. Limited understanding of value compared to competitors.
3. Lack of visibility into how and why prices are set.
4. Lack of insights into the negotiation games that customers play.

It's a mistake to blame the commercial teams. Sales professionals are the victims of a combination of internal and external forces. The internal forces are represented by cumbersome internal processes and shortsighted incentive structures that undermine price discipline. Poker-playing customers that are discerning and savvier than ever constitute the external forces. Businesses can learn to empower commercial teams to be champions of price and deliver on their company's potential. The objective is to close sales at profitable prices without leaving money on the table. How does the company leadership team change behavior to enable salespeople to be champions?

Four Steps to Building Sales Champions

Let's consider four steps to arm salespeople to realize value and better price:

Rational Individual Performance Goals   When salespeople have any level of control over price, are compensated (even partially) on volume, or are pushed to close an important sale too soon, they are incented to squander valuable profits to accomplish their mission.

The incentive mismatch problem goes beyond salespeople. Product and factory managers, who are compensated to keep the factory assembly lines moving or to achieve revenue or market share goals, and the tactics managers use at quarter-end can put pressure on pricing sales teams to close last-minute deals by dropping price.

Senior executives are often the worst offenders—especially those executives who are only incented to meet quarterly revenue objectives. Customers delight in leveraging this end-of-quarter desperation to get a better price.

Build Sales Confidence in the Company and the Financial Value Created for Customers   Ask salespeople how they feel about the products and services they sell. Often what we hear from salespeople is: our products and services are commodities. This may be because customers, whose sole agenda is to set the stage for getting lower prices, reinforce or "pound" this message into salespeople at every chance. They want sellers to know there are plenty of "good enough" alternatives.

While savvy companies understand and correctly dismiss these claims as negotiation ploys, too many other companies don't help salespeople defend their value to the customer. Instead, they allow the customer to set the price and then react to the fallout.

For many sellers, gaining confidence comes from knowing that they are selling better products and services that deliver more value than competitors.

Make Price Easy to Understand and Support   To most salespeople, discriminating between price strategies is a black box. They are not clear on why the price is the price and how it compares to a competitor. Internally, sales, marketing, and pricing teams that are siloed may disagree over the value of their products/services, and infighting on price becomes a time-consuming step in every deal. Sellers start internally negotiating to get their best customers lower prices.

Strive for simple, easy to understand pricing that documents the factors that determine current prices and levels. Importantly, highlight the differences from competitors' products if prices are higher. Prices and price strategy must be summarized simply and transparently.

The better a salesperson understands why the specific price is set, the better they can explain and defend the price during customer conversations. One successful company put their pricing organization on the road with salespeople. Their job was to present the basis for the price strategy and actively collaborate with sellers to determine how best to make it successful in winning deals. It worked well and both teams are now better collaborators on process and outcomes.

Help Salespeople Identify Negotiations Tactics and Prepare Correct Responses   Price negotiations are often a wild guess, and after some back and forth, the closing price comes in at a distance from the initial target. Because salespeople consider their real job as taking care of their best customers, giving great discounts often is part of that customer service. They have not had the deep value and budgetary impact conversations along the way.

When the salesperson arrives at procurement's office, they are blindsided by sophisticated negotiation tactics buyers have spent years developing. The salesperson may think the customer will be so upset with the offered price that they fold quickly and think they have saved the relationship. In these cases, salespeople may completely miss the cues in negotiating games that customers play and end up discounting too much. (See Rule Nine: Build Your Selling Backbone.)

A global information services company came to us because it experienced a significant trend in shrinking margins due to widespread discounting. The company introduced its sales team to value conversation training that helped decode customer behavior. By recognizing buyers' tactics and with newfound confidence in their ability to hold their ground, salespeople were able to counter requests for price concessions and negotiate win-win deals. In one outstanding instance, a customer showed a salesperson what purported to be a competitor's bid for one million dollars less. Instead of taking the bait, the newly inspired salesperson defended the company's price by demonstrating the value and differences in their proposal. The salesperson won the deal.

Price Strategy in a Recession

When a recession hits, demand declines. In a recession, the market growth projections anticipated by businesses are no longer tenable. Even so, companies initially respond to declines in volume by lowering prices in order to sell more products and services, desperately trying to meet gross revenue goals. This strategy is rarely effective. The problem is that other competitors are doing the same thing. They are all chasing business that is declining with lower prices, which leads to declines in revenue and dramatic declines in profit. Smart companies recognize this death spiral as a race to the bottom. Our advice is simple: never try to chase demand that because of a recession simply isn't there. The superior strategy is to adjust objectives, reset financial projections, eliminate unnecessary costs, and ride out the recession with your most profitable customers.

In reality, it isn't an issue of pricing in a recession. If you wait until recession is a reality to adjust price strategy, you are being reactive. A price strategy must be defined before a recession and in times when one might be coming. A system in place that tracks the likelihood of a recession or other market trends helps to execute the right plan at the right time. As a pricer, have a plan in place for what to do when the recession hits. It helps to have some leading indicators (such as end-use market growth) so you can get everyone ready to implement a revised plan.

CHAPTER 6

Rule Six

Innovate for Growth

Innovation is the lifeblood of successful organizations. New innovation meets the evolving needs of customers and focuses the organization to stay ahead of competitors. It provides a platform for Give-Gets to power win-win negotiations. When products are regarded as commodities, new services can serve to differentiate products and prop up prices.

Pricing is critical to businesses, but it's not the most vital thing. Businesses need to grow. Like sharks, which must keep moving to stay alive, businesses need forward momentum in the form of innovative products and services, expanding markets, and new opportunities for revenue and profit. Without such momentum, businesses cannot flourish. A disciplined pricing strategy is an important means to that end. But leaders must not be distracted from the main goal: deploying innovation to boost revenues and profits. Strategic pricing will help capture the value that your business creates, but without something to capture, even the most brilliant pricing strategy can't help you.

Without new products and services in the pipeline, businesses are reduced to having one lever to drive growth—price. These businesses push for higher prices in the hope that their customers will accept the price increases. The fear, of course, is that customers will bolt in the face of direct price increases. Some businesses try to finesse the issue by implementing back-door price increases in the form of layered fees and service charges. This has happened in banking and financial services and is currently happening in the shipping business.

Should Innovation Continue During Inflationary Market Conditions?

Innovation may be the most powerful deflationary force in the world. Artificial intelligence, for example, is dramatically reducing training time and costs. Inflation should justify more, not less, incentives for R&D. That's because only emerging technology allows businesses to satisfy the market's demand for goods and services. The efficient scalability delivered by innovation outpacing present and future demand may be the only force keeping prices from increasing. Moreover, innovation in the form of automation reduces the demand for labor, the largest fraction of any organization's cost structure, and makes retained workers more efficient.

Innovation happens on a continuum. It can be incremental (a cool new feature on a smartphone camera) or completely disruptive (self-driving cars). Smart companies operate at both ends of the continuum. When employees have an innovative mindset, they are full partners in the exploration of innovative ideas and customer inputs. One strategy is to use existing products to enter new markets where there may be fewer inflationary issues.

Inflation and market volatility give the makers of products and services perceived as indispensable more pricing power. For example, ASML, a Netherlands-based semiconductor equipment manufacturer, has a monopoly on Extreme Ultraviolet (EUV) lithography, a necessary technology for the fabrication of the advanced microchips that power everything from iPhones and cars to jet fighters and blenders.

ASML sells to the three largest semiconductor companies in the world. In technical terms, it's a triopsony, an economic condition in which there are only three large buyers for a specific product or service. Limited competition means the three buyers dictate market demand and hence enjoy outsize bargaining power over prices. It's usually not an ideal situation for the selling company.

But because semiconductor manufacturers are under intense pressure from their own customers to increase supply, the market leaders such as Intel, Broadcom, and Qualcomm are desperate for higher production capacity. In such circumstances, ASML is in the driver's seat on pricing. ASML now demands premium prices not just for its current production but for guaranteed consignment of future production.

Innovate for Growth, Price for Profits

To break the cycle, innovate for growth and price for profits. To improve your pricing leverage, some element of your offerings must be differentiated. Otherwise, they are commodities, and the lowest price gets the business. The challenge for many firms is that their core offerings are commodities—or close to it. That's fine. There are customers that have basic needs. For the rest of your markets, differentiating from the competition is vital. In addition to high-value products, greater differentiation can derive from services.

The global steel industry is a great setting to see how this plays out. Steel, a technology developed around 1000 BC, is as pure a commodity as one can find. Large global competitors are buying up smaller basic steel plants around the world with the aim of dominating price-based competition. Yet niche opportunities for premium prices abound. Argentina's Tenaris SA provides high-value seamless steel pipes used in offshore drilling operations around the world—an application enjoying soaring demand as the petroleum industry moves farther offshore.

The growth of this market makes it attractive for the global giants, who can offer low prices to customers. In contrast Tenaris bundles high-value-added services with its premium steel pipes—a strategy that has been effective at keeping these global giants out of the market. Tenaris bundles advanced technical support, engineering, and just-in-time deliveries that help its customers improve their exploration and production operations. Their understanding of the way their customers operate—economically, technologically, and environmentally—differentiates them from the price-oriented steel conglomerates.

The net result: Tenaris and other niche players are able to command and protect prices of $2,000 per ton, over three times the prices the global commodity players battle over. Their understanding of customer operations and priorities enables them to gain far higher profitability margins and keep the titans at bay.

Sources of Innovation

There is no magic about where to find innovation. Customers know what is needed next. A good value-based approach to customer relationships identifies wide ranges of ideas for feature, product, and service innovations which customers value. The trick is to make sure they are willing to pay for the innovation as part of the discovery process. Then you have an idea of both the value of the innovation to them and the viability of the innovation for your business. There are four types of innovations to consider:

1. **Incremental Innovation** involves feature/service improvements of existing products into existing markets.
2. **Disruptive Innovation** is the development of modern technologies for your existing markets.

3. Architectural Innovation takes existing technology to new markets to expand a business globally.
4. Radical Innovation is the development of innovative technologies for new markets.

We fervently hope that the days are over of sending a team of technologists to the laboratory with the hopes that they'll yell "eureka" and produce your next silver bullet of growth.

Polaroid was a technological leader in instant photography using specialty chemicals. They were quite successful and knew full well that digital photography was the wave of the future. So they applied their chemical process to instant movies. Polaroid's Polavision was introduced at the same time as the first video cassette recorders (VCRs) were coming out. Introduced at a higher price with a lower quality, Polavision quickly hit the scrap heap of inwardly-focused innovation. We had a conversation with the chief engineer at Kodak where he scoffed at the failure of one of their competitors. He was blindsided several years later when Kyocera introduced the first camera phone.

Incremental innovation provides many opportunities for the innovative evolution of a business and your customer experience. Conduct interviews with non-customers to get ideas as well. Innovation for non-customers provides an excellent opportunity to expand your competitive footprint using value rather than price.

Innovation During Inflationary Times

Innovation and inflation tend to be asynchronous. That is, high inflation represents an impediment to the imperative of innovation. It's not hard to see why. Whatever the level of resource a firm dedicates to innovation, inflation tilts any commitment away from innovative activities and toward return-dominated programs. The result, more or less, is a reduction in innovation and long-term growth. According to a recent study by the World Bank, a one percentage point increase in inflation reduces the establishment-level probability of innovation by 4.3% (Evers, Niemann, and Schiffbauer, 2018, "Inflation, liquidity and innovation," Policy Research Working Paper Series 8436, The World Bank).

Constant inflation is a siren's song of growth for a company. Costs go up, prices go up, and all is good in the eyes of the captains of industry. When inflation wanes, as it inevitably will, businesses crash on the rocks when they believe that their only engine of growth is price. When other competitors, which were pursuing the same approach, discover the same thing, you end up with entire industries that decline into a price war that benefits no one. Well, not "no one"; in the short term, purchasing agents love and encourage the process because they are getting lower prices.

We had one client that got fed up with this cycle and decided to reduce the capacity of the industry and only serve customers that were willing to pay for "reliability of supply" in what was generally thought to be a highly commoditized market. The result was almost comical. They advised customers what was coming. They implemented price increases and took one plant and converted production to another "commodity." Their primary competitors agreed to pick up demand and quickly stumbled, leaving those customers with no supply. Needless to say, the customers that had left came running back with their tails between their legs and bought at significantly higher prices. The client discovered that all of their "price buying" customers (Rule Nine: Build Your Selling Backbone) had been playing poker with them for decades.

Prudent companies track growth that comes from four sources:

1. Growth from price increases—with a deep understanding of those increases which are used to cover costs and those that reflect a better job of capturing value.
2. Growth from new products and services.
3. Growth from new markets.
4. Organic Growth from acquisitions.

Firms that can successfully track growth across these four dimensions usually have a clearer understanding and goal structure for both salespeople, commercial pursuit teams, and technical teams for profitable growth in each area. While they are currently facing inflationary times, one approach, of course, is to increase prices to reflect both increasing costs and supply chain problems. At the same time, the trick is to make sure they are also assessing and developing for goals in those other areas as well. This book argues that more effective strategies exist.

The Problem with Using Price to Drive Growth

During inflationary times, pricing is often the primary tool to drive growth. Even during extended periods of stability, we see firms that rely exclusively on price to drive the growth of the firm. That's dangerous since, if you think about what we discussed in Rule Five: Strategy Sets the Direction, there are many cases, dictated by the market, of competitive and customer reliance where the use of price as a tool for growth can lead to declines in sales and dramatic decline in profits. An overreliance on pricing to drive growth damages relationships with your customers.

As an example, the air cargo business is a brutally competitive sector driven by price. The air cargo carriers have learned that they can be competitive on published rates but only if they tack on an array of fees for fuel, inspections, and a host of other service costs. For the time being, air cargo companies enjoy a critical mass of loyal customers who regard the air cargo companies as logistics partners. High switching costs currently make it impractical for many customers to abandon their existing air cargo partners. But as billing becomes more transparent and customers absorb the impact of these fees, many customers will bolt.

Luckily, there's a practical solution to avoid the vicious cycle. Businesses create options to present a dual-level bundling approach that has a low-price, bare-bones offering and a higher-price, full-service offering. This solution prevents alienation of loyal customers and also gives salespeople some choices to offer poker-playing buyers to better ferret out their position. In most markets, as we will see in Rule Nine, there are more value- or relationship-oriented customers than price-oriented customers. If it often doesn't seem like that, it's because procurement professionals have learned to act like price buyers in order to get greater discounts. More detail is available in Chapter Nine (Build Your Selling Backbone).

The Basics of a Good Offering Structure

To create high-impact offerings, set out some basic objectives. The basic objectives include:

- Matching offerings with the high-value needs of target customer segments.
- Offering low-value flanking products that appeal to price-sensitive customers and reduce the effects of price negotiations on high-value offerings.
- Meeting or beating competitive performance on core customer needs.
- Building strong fences between high- and low-value offerings to prevent customers from negotiating for high-value offerings at low prices.

- Training salespeople on how to have clear discussions with customers with choices that define price-value trade-offs during negotiations (Rule Eight).
- Arming sales with Give-Gets, well-defined product/service levers to alter offering value and price by adding or removing specific features.

An essential benefit of well-defined offering levels is that it enables your sales teams to better control price negotiations. Having both high- and low-value offerings puts sales in the driver's seat during price negotiations. If they are pressured to lower the price, they can offer the customer the low-value product. For some, the low-value offering will better meet their needs and budget, so they'll buy it. On the other hand, most poker-playing customers will react with indignation. They do this because the salesperson has called their bluff and exposed their true intention: getting the high-value offering for a low price.

The reality of managing this poker game is that it is a little bit more complicated than just having one high-value and one low-value offering. After all, you have multiple segments with different use cases to serve. And each customer within those segments may have varying needs. Setting up sales to control the poker game and better manage pricing requires creating more options for price-value trade-offs. To do this, it is helpful to think of constructing offerings with three levels: core offerings, expected offerings, and value-added options. Let's consider each in turn.

Value-Added Options: The Critical Role of Services and Solutions

Even though the logic of high- to low-value product offerings is compelling, it is not enough. Most firms are facing commoditization of their core products. Finding it harder to stay ahead of the competition, the smart ones have invested heavily in creating value-added options: services, consulting operations, and capabilities for outsourcing entire business processes.

Those firms that succeed create a cadre of loyal customers, competitive barriers, and confidence in their prices because they are creating superior value for their customers. Some of the service innovators have been at it a long time. Traditional product companies like GE and Air Products began developing their successful models many years ago.

Developing Services and Solutions to Create Pricing Leverage

Let's start by categorizing services. The first category is enabling services such as maintenance and support, postdelivery training, or predelivery design support. These types of services are often expected to be available, and that expectation is often misinterpreted as an unwillingness to pay for them. The rationalization to give them away is almost always the same: "We have to include those services to ensure that the product performs." But customers will pay for them, and, accordingly, they should be an explicit part of the offering and price menus.

When sellers feel these services must be included, ask two basic questions. First, "At what level should our services perform?" Second, "What is the monetary impact for customers if there are different levels of performance?" The answers to these questions do two things. They force a definition of the boundaries between the expected and value-added levels for services, and they enable identification of customers and which are seeking high or low value. The second category of services are high-value adds and are often components of solutions to specific customer business problems.

Combining enabling services and value-add services can lead to the creation of powerful solutions for customers. Consider General Electric and its design of the GE90 aircraft engine. The GE90 was a modern design competing against older offerings from Pratt & Whitney and Rolls-Royce. Using new materials and engineering advances, the GE90 was a technological marvel. But at the beginning of the GE90's development, it was also a commercial failure.

What happened? It turns out that GE hadn't done its homework in the area of customer value. While its engines were technically superior, GE, to its surprise, lost deal after deal to Pratt & Whitney and Rolls-Royce. The reason, as GE eventually discovered, was simple. Customers were reluctant to take the risk of change. They chose a product they knew over a product they didn't because with experience came predictable total costs of ownership.

GE responded by creating an entire solution around the GE90 that simultaneously addressed customers' financial concerns (their value needs) while demonstrating the competitive advantages of the engine's feature set. The new solution called "Power by the Hour" tapped into the old practice of leasing capital equipment so that customers could pay for a fully maintained and operational engine.

Logical, Disciplined Offering Structure

When we talk with product teams about the importance of low-value flanking products and value-adding services, they express two very real concerns. The first is fear that if they introduce a low-value option that it will cannibalize demand for their higher-value offerings. And second, they will not be able to control access to services. If either of these happens, it could wreak havoc with their P&L. The key to addressing both concerns is to create a series of fences to protect the organization from such threats.

One of the main reasons for having a logical, disciplined offering structure is to prevent customers from obtaining high-value offerings for unjustified low prices. The basic elements of the offering structure must enable the creation of fences to work. A fence is just what it sounds like: a means to protect the integrity of offerings by forcing a trade-off between price and value. An effective strategy for market dominance is to develop a dual offering that covers both the high- and low-end customer needs. Flanking offerings both grow the revenue and protect the global footprint of the firm.

Creating good fences is another one of those overlooked areas where product teams can build value for their organizations. The key is to pick criteria that will withstand all-out assaults by poker-playing customers and will be supported by senior leaders. Common examples of strong fences include distinct differences in product features, sales channels, service and support levels, logistics, and brand. Providers of information products use timeliness of access, depth of information, ability to perform analysis, catalog data, and format. The good news is that the rules for creating actionable fences are simple.

1. Fences must be based on clear, objective criteria.
2. The criteria must make sense to both customers and the sales professionals.

This transparency allows you to pass the ultimate test and explain to one customer how and why another customer qualified for a lower price. Confidence in pricing allows sales professionals to justify differentiation in pricing without any of the pain and suffering when challenged as to why another customer is getting a lower price.

Building Pricing Leverage

The differentiation in product and service offerings is often the most underutilized asset in building pricing leverage. And if product and services are haphazardly allowed to evolve, key offerings lose definition and differentiation is diluted. They also lose their unique value. Confusion reigns, pricing integrity suffers, and returns on investments in development and innovation are diminished.

Organizations over this hurdle take actions that are distinctly different. They are rigorous about connecting customer value insights to tightly defined offerings. They use combinations of products, services, and solutions to create offering levers for their sales teams to control negotiations. They have found the critical connection between pricing models, price lists, and offering structure. Offering architecture defines the possibilities and limits of what can be done in pricing.

CHAPTER 7

Rule Seven

Understand Your Market

To optimize pricing strategy, businesses need a clear and current understanding of markets: the behavior of customers and competitors in the context of the Four Ps (product, price, place, promotion). Moreover, markets are continually influenced by variables such as supply shortages, economic shocks, inflation, labor volatility, pandemics, and wars. Knowing how to respond to each variable is the key to pricing success.

Inflation can be a benefit for businesses that understand their customers, appreciate the value they deliver, connect that value with the go-to needs of the customers, and are nimble enough to act quickly in the face of rapidly evolving business conditions. For businesses lulled into complacency by years of operating in stable economic conditions, inflation can be an existential threat. In this chapter, we'll focus on the market triggers of inflation on pricing and how businesses can prepare themselves.

Over time, inflation significantly impacts every market pricing decision. Inflation has many causes, but the two main triggers are demand-pull and cost-push. Demand-pull inflation happens when an increase in the demand for goods and services leads producers to raise prices to maximize profits.

Markets are the playing field on which enterprises evaluate their strategy and tactics for delivering value. The elements of the strategy include decisions about price, terms and conditions, sourcing, and customer service. An understanding of each of these elements with respect to the unique circumstances of each customer is required if a business is to defend prices and enhance competitive position, profits, and revenue.

No Magic Bullet

There is no magic silver bullet to "fix" inflation through pricing. What disciplined pricing can do is to maintain profitability in an inflationary market. Strategic implementation calls for the discipline to deploy the necessary offering levers and activate them at the right time for the right purposes. Carefully managed, the levers of pricing can even result in growth that eluded the enterprise under more stable economic conditions. The most critical element of discipline is organizational nimbleness. Enterprises must be capable of acting rapidly, selectively raising prices before rising costs deteriorate profitability.

For our clients struggling with inflationary challenges, we specifically recommend building muscle in the six following areas.

Know Thy Market

What's causing the market volatility in your specific sector? That's the most critical question to answer. While it's useful to understand the various causes of general inflation, it's more important to differentiate the causes specifically confronting your sector.

Just to review, there are two main causes of inflation: demand-pull and cost-push. Demand-pull inflation is seen when an increase in the demand for goods and services causes producers to raise prices to maintain profitability. Cost-push inflation occurs when producers raise prices because their costs have gone up.

Labor shortages represent another example of demand-pull inflation. We saw nationwide examples of how employers struggled with hiring in the wake of the COVID-19 pandemic. As employers recovered and needed workers, they found that the wages that were acceptable pre-pandemic were suddenly no longer sufficient to lure workers back to the job. As demand for workers outstripped supply, wages increased, adding to inflationary pressures. As labor unit costs account for, depending on the industry, as much as 70% of total business costs wages, wage instability creates enormous planning problems.

Other common causes of inflation include rising fuel and transportation costs, labor shortages, and an expanding economy. (In the latter case, inflation is considered a positive. Indeed, the Federal Reserve aims for a 2% annual core inflation rate; the only thing worse than inflation is deflation.) Analysts point to the expansion of the money supply, servicing the national debt, and government regulation as incremental causes of inflation. These are just additional instances of cost-push inflation.

So the first thing to understand is what's causing the market volatility in your sector. The follow-up is to determine whether this volatility is a short-term or long-term issue. For example, assume that the causes complicating your ability to serve your customers are labor shortages down the value chain. Now, is this a short-term or long-term issue? Your answer will dictate your response.

One of our clients, the CEO of a transportation company, has taken the position that inflation is a long-term issue. Market volatility and supply chain constraints, he estimates, will last for years. His analysis of the transportation market recognizes a structural issue: the existing supply chain that lumbered along in stable market conditions was simply not prepared for the instability caused by the pandemic. As consumers shifted buying behavior from retail stories to ecommerce sales, the supply chain could not keep up with the increasing labor market for home delivery services. This fundamental shift, the CEO concluded, was one of many factors in the labor shortage and could not be classified as a short-term issue.

Understand Your Customers

This is an opportune time to review your customers on the dimensions that matter most. And perhaps the key dimension is profitability. Businesses often grow by accepting every customer that comes along. The businesses often distort their product offerings and even sales territories to meet new customer demands. Over time and business mergers, companies inherit a disjointed customer base where it is unclear which customers are profitable to serve and which are not.

The customer review is essentially a measure of how profitable a particular customer currently is. The review compares revenue (how much revenue a specific customer generates) against costs (how much is spent on customer acquisition and every touchpoint of service, as measured in direct costs and overhead).

The review often starts by segmenting new customers versus long-term customers. Customers on contract versus those that pay as they go is another important segmentation. In either case, the central challenge is to know the profitability of your top customers. We talked about this imperative in Rule Four (Know Your Value).

A fundamental question is: Can the organization provide value aligned with the cost to serve? Understanding these elements will help determine which customers provide profit to the firm and warrant additional investment to develop. The customers that fall to the bottom 20% of profitability should create an action plan designed to improve profitability and reset expectations such as their priority to receive products and services until increased profitability warrants a step-up in service. Without movement in these areas, it occasionally becomes incumbent upon a business to part ways with a customer.

The next question is whether a specific customer poses a risk to the organization. Prioritize risky contracts and develop an action plan to remove elements of uncertainty by including new language that adjusts prices automatically based on external justifications such as indexes commercial businesses are familiar with. The Consumer Price Index (CPI) is a commonly referenced metric based on a basket of goods and services measured by the Bureau of Labor & Statistics. A less commonly known index is the Personal Consumption Expenditures (PCE) Index. The CPI measures the change in the out-of-pocket expenditures of all urban households while the PCE index measures the change in goods and services consumed by all households, and nonprofit institutions serving households. The PCE index is used by the Federal Reserve to make interest rate decisions. The Produce Price Index (PPI) is similar to CPI but measures prices of goods and services used by businesses to create goods for consumers.

Once the measure of inflation is agreed upon within the organization, proactively adjust and refine your business to maintain profitability. It might mean shuttering a plant or a product portfolio or making price adjustments in others. Not all costs change at the same rate, so be specific about which products and services are selected for increases. With all of this happening, it is important to give customers choices. They won't like being backed into a corner, so it is important to understand their budget and likely constraints and have two or three options.

When talking about these changes with customers, provide evidence, justification, and be definitive. This is the health of your company. At the same time remind them of the value you provide and your commitment to continue to provide value.

Part of understanding your market is a deep-rooted understanding of your customers. One company told us that a differentiator for them has been service levels. They found out early in this market that service levels are much more important than product value. They invested more heavily in their services and further differentiated themselves from the competition and now price services are higher than others. They were able to be proactive here because they invest time in understanding their customers' changing needs.

Align with Long-Term Customer Needs and Add Value

Customers are smart so don't use inflation as an excuse to raise prices across the board. Customers know market conditions, they are expecting higher prices, supply chain issues, and labor shortages. Be honest, transparent, and confident.

- Increase value of solutions through bundling to increase price.
- Change price metrics to better align with value accrual. Consider potential risk share agreements with high risk/profitable customers.
- Change price model to reflect when the customers' end-users may run out of budget or demand slows. For example, a country CEO at an IT distributor focused on a shift in the business model when end-user demand cooled off because

the higher prices would eat up budgets at a higher rate. Next, he will get ready for end-users to move a subscription business such as hardware-as-a-service.

- Instill good governance to manage price and customer expectations.

Prepare for Growth Early

During inflationary times, there could be an opportunity for large strategic decisions through mergers and acquisitions (M&A) if the cost of capital is still reasonable. Some of our clients have taken this opportunity to get more vertically integrated by buying a key supplier. This allows for risk mitigation as well as competitive advantage. Others have chosen to buy smaller competitors to expand their portfolio and enter new markets that may potentially be less volatile. Another beneficial use of capital is to diversify your supply chain by adding more countries and doing near-shoring based on future demand clusters.

Before choosing any of these strategies, make sure that you take the time to understand your customers and what they will need over time, not just what they need today. Especially in volatile markets, a customer's value drivers tend to change more often so it is important to understand this before choosing a long-term M&A play.

Know Thy Competitor

Competitors are unavoidable in business today. It makes doing business more difficult. But, if we're honest, we will acknowledge that the competition is good for markets. It helps participants keep the focus on innovation, efficiency, and value.

The weakness we have with competitors is our attitude. We compete fairly; they cheat. Our prices are fair; their prices are predatory. We conclude that they are either fiendishly clever or behaving irrationally. In short, we vilify the competition, assigning them sinister motives for behavior not much different than our own. Does this sound familiar?

Somehow, we rarely consider that competitors think about us precisely the same way we think about them. Our attitude about competition justifies much of our destructive behavior, such as rampant price discounting. Attitude causes us to pull the price trigger too often. It causes us to get into negotiations that we should walk away from. Our attitude causes us to lose pricing power.

We need to change this sense of powerlessness and replace it with confidence. The best advice ever is 3,000 years old. "The best general enters the mind of his enemy," wrote Lao Tzu in the *Tao Te Ching*. To be more successful in our markets and with our customers, we need to do a better job of understanding our competitors. We must understand what they are doing, what their next move may be, and why they are likely to make that move.

Be Proactive

One trick when you are in a deal with competitors is to be proactive. When a competitor senses you are in reactive mode, they will attack in a place where they have the most to gain and you have the most to lose. What if you stop playing catch-up and take the lead? Could you take the fight to them in another region or with a customer where they have the most to lose and you have the most to gain? Do so with nimble assurance and you are less likely to get hurt. Also, it is less likely there will be a damaging price war. To get there takes a system of understanding and responding properly to competitors. Whether by matching price or making a public announcement, the intent is to minimize the damage of price competition.

Intuit ranked number eleven on *Fortune Magazine's* 2021 list of the influential "100 Best Places to Work," develops personal finance and tax software. Based in Mountain View, California, the company continues to dominate its markets despite the fact that Microsoft, among many other players, has been a competitor for years. Microsoft even made a failed bid to buy Intuit in the 1990s. Microsoft is 20 times the size of Intuit and has plenty of cash to go after Intuit's lucrative markets. Yet Intuit stays ahead by relentlessly innovating based on its understanding of its customers' needs. It does a superior job of introducing low-cost, entry-level products. It follows this with outstanding customer service. It maintains excellent relationships with the two hundred thousand accountants in the U.S. who are key buying influences.

Intuit proactively anticipates what Microsoft and its other competitors will do next. It tries to make sure its own development resources are focused in the most desirable areas. Intuit realizes that Microsoft will continue to target the small business accounting market. It has developed a number of scenarios on the potential impact Microsoft can make. This intelligence allows Intuit to keep developing and pre-announcing new products that keep Microsoft off-balance. It uses nimbleness as an advantage. Intuit has entered the mind of its competitor and has prospered.

Intuit doesn't just react to Microsoft; it out-innovates Microsoft. Intuit knows that if it were forced to go head-to-head with Microsoft, it would lose. The goal is to keep its larger competitor off-balance and in perpetual catch-up mode. And they do it not with price but with relentless innovation of their products and services. Intuit's nimbleness limits Microsoft's ability to use price alone to elbow its way into the market. It's an example of how to use product and service innovations to stay ahead of competitors that you can't beat in a price-driven conflict.

In summary, when competitive action is needed, make it quick. Have well-considered game plans for expected contingencies that are focused not on beating competitors but on getting them off your back. Take the example of PeopleSoft and Oracle. The two competitors tried to beat each other in every way, including price. They both gave massive discounts to customers who adopted their high-value enterprise software, but in doing so, they both left lots of money on the table. As a last resort, one competitor acquires the other. PeopleSoft eventually lost the battle when Oracle acquired it. What happened next? Oracle promptly raised prices.

Market Changes from the Coronavirus

The *Wall Street Journal* has had numerous reports about businesses struggling with pricing during the pandemic. Like many pricing consultancies, we are receiving numerous calls from companies struggling with declining sales they attribute to inflation. They want to know if they can solve the problem of declining sales by increasing prices. In general, we tell them, the answer is "no." Blindly increasing prices across-the-board in a vacuum just makes the problem worse.

Consider a business whose customers are intensely sensitive to pricing: the aviation industry. Inflation hammers airlines as their two most significant cost centers—fuel and labor—are rising faster than general inflation. Many airlines are concluding that their current revenue management models aren't working anymore. Why? Because demand has dropped. The pandemic has caused an important segment of the flying public—leisure travelers—to dramatically reduce the number of flights they book.

To make matters worse, the pandemic caused the most profitable segment of flying customers—business travelers—to change their behaviors. Remote work and videoconferencing have replaced many in-person events that required business travel. The benefits are so compelling that even as the pandemic wanes, many business events will continue to be delivered virtually. These changes in consumer buying behavior represent an existential threat to the airline industry unless it changes the way it models its business analytics. Airlines traditionally look at historical data coming out of a limited number of geographical segments. But historical market segmentation data isn't going to help airlines deal with pandemic-driven exceptional circumstances.

Dax Cross, CEO of Revenue Analytics, likens relying on historical data to flying with "blinders on." The solution requires a better understanding, in real time, of customers, their fears, their desires, and how they behave. Traditional segmentation doesn't work because it groups dissimilar customers without distinction. What's required is for airlines to do analytics on smaller, more relevant groups of customers or cohorts. With good analytics and dashboards summarizing the results, the market segments can be evaluated to see how they respond to pricing variables. The mathematicians refer to this process as "stochastic analysis." We prefer the term "cohort analysis." It's remarkably effective at teasing out the differences in the behavior of discrete customer segments.

We are impressed with a number of businesses, which responded well to the challenges of the pandemic when agility is worth its weight in gold. A raw materials supplier impressed us with its ability to make price changes in sub-second timing. The company's entire business model relies on managing risks by being able to implement quick price changes based on real-time market volatility.

The executive here told us the key to being able to manage pricing during periods of price volatility is by using a portfolio methodology. The executive identified the elements of the portfolio: channel, pricing strategies, product, and services pricing, as well as price types (e.g., flat pricing, indexed pricing, and multi-variable pricing). The executive recommended tools to spread the market risks by partnering with other providers in the channel facing similar risks. This kind of collaboration helps mitigate risks and increases the value to the end-user.

Such collaboration with channel partners not only mitigates risk but represents real differentiation. Throughout this process, the executive reminded us of the importance of lowering costs through a combination of automation. Finally, businesses must invest in their most profitable customers and divest, at all costs, those customers who cannot be served at a profit.

Customer Response to Price Change

When thinking about a market, start with customers. It's true that some customers in mature B2B relationships will switch their suppliers based on price, but they don't increase their volumes as a result. If pricers plan to drop price to increase demand they will frequently be disappointed. Customers make it look like they are willing to switch for a lower price, but they don't actually buy any more products. This reality frustrates suppliers who think they are lowering prices as a competitive advantage. The discounting merely results in price wars in which the only winner is the customer.

Remember the discussion of derived demand in Rule Five: Strategy Sets the Direction? When competitors keep lowering price to accommodate the willingness of customers to switch, they reduce their revenue and, in many cases, eliminate any profits. The problem is that many managers confuse that activity for market elasticity, where markets actually grow as a result of the lower prices. In this case, the customer did not offer the vendors any additional volume. They offered nothing in return for the lower price. When employing a discount, the payoff should be to get something of value for the concession: a Give-Gets (See Rule Eight: Build Your Give-Gets Muscles). Any other use of a discount just reduces revenue and often eliminates profits.

Yes, sometimes a company decides to drop prices to close an order. But when it does, two adverse things invariably result. First, customers are now trained to negotiate even harder next time. Second, the company leaves money on the table. So, before using price discounts, consider whether customers are going to incrementally buy more of your products or services. If not, the company may be better off not discounting and relying on better selling of tangible value. In this case, it should create trusses for more backbone in the selling process.

Are You Playing Chess or Checkers?

Pricing dynamics can be thought of in the context of games. For example, one of our clients reacted when a competitor made a move into their market space. The client's initial inclination was to play checkers; that is, to respond by simply matching the competitor's prices. When clients are in reactive mode and tactically focus on only the move ahead of them, we call that playing checkers.

In these cases, we generally counsel patience to avoid the over-reaction that comes with taking action for the sake of taking action. After persuading the client to get over the need to "do something and do it fast," we had the space to perform a proper analysis of the true implications of the competitive intrusion. Our analysis demonstrated that the intrusion was not as much of a threat as the client believed. The competitor's products were inferior. More importantly, the market perceived the competitor's distribution system as inadequate and problematic. We recognized that the proper response was not to match the prices of the competitor. The better response for the client was to strengthen its value messaging and protect its supply chain.

That realization led the client to shore up that supply chain with extended contracts that included price and revenue guarantees that resulted in long-term exclusive commitments. This made conditions precarious for the competitor. Rather than weakening their position by trying to compete on price, our client protected its position. The upshot? Wonderful increases in both revenue and profitability.

By taking an analytical approach, our client graduated to playing chess. They came to understand the potential moves of a competitor and responded in a holistic way. They minimized the damage of the competitive intrusion, limited the options of the competitor, and strengthened their own position for the near future.

As you consider the implications of Know Thy Market in the context of your own pricing dynamics, ask yourself this question. Are you playing checkers or chess? Along the way, be aware of disruptions to your pricing strategy from any number of random shocks, some of which can be anticipated, while others—Black Swan events—cannot be predicted. Regardless, managers who respond quickly and effectively minimize the damage.

Building the Global Chessboard

To price with confidence, companies target the right customers and the right segments. Once the strategy is set, there is a simple tool that can be used to communicate the direction the commercial team can take to execute effectively. We call it the Global Price Strategy Chessboard. The chessboard helps managers map their efforts to checkmate a competitor in a manner that is agreed on by company leaders. It reduces conflict and anxiety and gets everyone working in the same direction with their time and discount resources.

Figure 7.1 is an example of the discount grid. The grid provides the backdrop understanding that is critical for effective

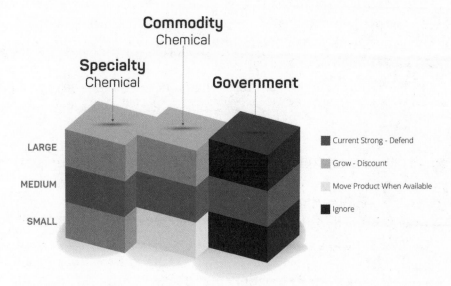

FIGURE 7.1   Global Price Strategy Chessboard

competitive information management. It contains the information on what to say and what to do with pricing and selling efforts. In its simplest form, as shown here, it takes a firm's primary segments or geographies and customers (in this case based on size) and prioritizes them.

In this case, there are four simple priorities. Let's consider four segments called current strong, grow, move product, and ignore.

- In the current strong segments, the company has a strong market position and there is little it can do to extend its market position without causing a price war. The decision is to take care of this segment and defend, if necessary.

- The grow segments receive the majority of the discounts. The company might be growing, or it might be in an area where competitors are stronger. So the intent is to grow penetration in that segment.

- The move product segments highlight where the company can move product at low prices without upsetting the competitive balance in the industry. It should be made up primarily of price buyers, attractive only when the company has a bunch of excess capacity.

- The ignore segments represent customers who may be served if they want to meet the price. But if they want a discount, forget about it!

Look at what this grid does for everyone in the company. It identifies in a simple manner where and how to deal with customers—all of them. It puts a stake in the ground for where to discount. The grid shows managers where they should be spending their time and, perhaps more importantly, where they shouldn't be spending their time. It can be put together fairly quickly by the leadership of the firm. It meets one of the primary requirements of leadership: providing people direction. If managers don't do this, they will not effectively deal with conflicting agendas in the silos within the company. Companies that do this tend to execute strategy much more precisely.

Successful companies have a good understanding of who their competitors are and their strengths and weaknesses. Managers take those insights and instead of reacting directly to a competitor's moves, they determine strategically where and when to respond to those moves. They understand how to best respond in a way that doesn't turn the interaction into a customer or industry-level price war. When those insights and actions are turned into effective competitive information, they provide long-term competitive advantage that stops leaving money on the table in ineffective price battles in the wrong markets with the wrong competitors.

CHAPTER 8

Rule Eight

Build Your Give-Gets Muscle

Commercial teams successful in implementing effective price strategy exercise a powerful discipline or muscle that they can deploy on a regular basis. We call it Give-Gets, otherwise known as trade-offs. By whatever term, it means agreeing to a reduction in price coupled with a corresponding reduction in value to the customer. A fence prevents customers from getting access to features and services when they haven't paid for them. Product managers can protect value with the right fences. Customers give less so they get less. Give-Gets are the antidote to the traditional propensity to discount.

Using the Offering Structure to Win at the Negotiating Table

We have found that discounting is the greatest source of price leakage today. Customers feeling the weight of price increases during this inflationary time may push even harder for deeper discounts. While discounting is a cultural habit by many companies, it is only worse now. To stop the bleeding, the first action is commitment by all leaders within the company to stand behind the price. Give-Gets provide the fuel to maintain price value alignment. With rampant inflation, it is important to give customers choices instead of a straight up price increase. Offering choices will give your customer a stronger feeling of your partnership and care for their business.

In our business, clients often request a discount, and we usually agree. We are not against negotiating. But here's the kicker. We tie the discount to a reduction in the scope of the service to the client. The best negotiators know that if they pull the price lever, they must pull the value lever at the same time. That is, if the client expects to get something of value (a reduced fee), they must expect to give something of value, e.g., reduced scope of work, longer delivery time, lower value product, less favorable terms and conditions. We call this a "Give-Gets" dynamic.

Exercising Give-Gets should become your go-to response when customers request a reduction in price. They are little gems that can be used to deliver differentiated value benefits to customers. With Give-Gets, customers can more easily discriminate higher- and lower-value options. Ultimately, Give-Gets are another tool in the negotiations game to be played or pulled off the table as needed to close the deal.

Playing the Give-Gets hand accomplishes a number of important benefits. First, it changes the discussion at the negotiating table from price to value. Procurement people will bristle, of course. They often want to negotiate exclusively for lower prices and try to stay away from value because it undermines their ability to bluff you into discounting. Give-Gets muscle alerts the customer that they are going to incur a reduction in benefits when buying based on price alone.

There are endless ways for a company to exercise its Give-Gets muscle. Consider a manufacturer of industrial products, which is reeling from price increases of raw materials driven by inflation and transportation costs. The company announced a price increase. At the same time, it gave its best customers an opportunity to preserve existing prices in return for less generous terms and conditions. In order to preserve the existing price, the customer could, for example, agree to faster payment terms, e.g., from 30 days net to 15 days net. Or it could agree to increase its overall volume of purchases or even add additional products to their orders. Otherwise, the price increase would take effect.

Another client, a distributor, responded to the sudden increase in fuel prices by putting their customers on notice that it would impose a temporary fuel surcharge. While research shows that most customers accept well-communicated surcharges, one particular customer resisted the price increase. Fine, the distributor responded. For you, we won't impose a fuel surcharge. But our practice of sending you product in partial truck deliveries will have to stop. You will either need to wait until you order enough material to fill up a full load or dispatch your own truck. No more partial truck deliveries. The customer accepted the surcharge.

Dynamic Give-Gets

Sometimes Give-Gets are dynamic and play out when a company decides to implement a price increase by explicitly charging for a benefit that the customer previously received at no cost. Recognizing the value of such a service is one thing. Persuading the customer to accept the new pricing is another.

Give-Gets provides a solution. In this case, a fire equipment manufacturing company engaged us to advise them on how it could get its customers—fire stations—to accept a price increase. A little background: Fire stations are all about responding to emergencies quickly. One service that fire station managers value from their vendors is the ability to receive product quickly. The fire equipment company traditionally responded to this customer desire by holding equipment in inventory to meet demand. In other words, the company anticipated demand by holding in inventory the equipment that fire stations might need so when an order comes in, it can deliver the goods immediately.

Holding inventory is a risky, capital-intensive service. In inflationary times, such a service becomes even more risky. The study we conducted helped the company calculate the cost of holding inventory and understand the value it was providing by doing so. Once we did that, the service value to customers emerged. The company decided to charge extra for its ability to ship equipment immediately. If customers accepted the extra charges, they would be entitled to receive orders from inventory immediately. If a customer resisted the price increase, no problem. They would preserve the original price but would have to wait for the order to go through the normal procurement cycle. Most fire stations saw enough value in getting equipment quickly that they accepted the price increase.

Correlated to Reduction in Price

Give-Gets drive a reduction in costs that can correlate to the reduction in price. The point is to remain profitable. That said, don't spend a lot of time worrying about comparing the level of price change to the level of cost change. Yes, there has to be some correlation between the two, but it doesn't have to be precise. In fact, we've seen successful negotiations where the differential cost was virtually zero between the high- and low-value offering. The negotiations concerned a communications product. There were two versions. The first version had basic communications technology. The higher value product had advanced encryption and geo-location capabilities. The first product sold for $12,000; the second sold for $23,000. What was the cost difference? Activating a software "switch," which enabled the more valuable capabilities.

Recognize the structure of most negotiations in a B2B environment. The user and specifier are often removed from the negotiation. Instead, professional procurement people drive the negotiation. Recognize that the reason the user and specifier are absent is because customers know that procurement professionals can bluff more effectively when they are divorced from the teams that actually recognize the value the supplier provides. The question is whether the real users and decision makers will let procurement people change the companies they want to do business with.

Give-Gets don't work in a vacuum. They require everyone in the organization to agree on what they are, why they are important, under what conditions they are appropriate, and, perhaps more importantly, under what conditions they are not effective. Commercial teams must have leadership back the structure to help them conduct more powerful negotiations.

Give-Gets are, to a certain extent, the rules of engagement with customers. In Rule Ten (Deploy Three Practices to Increase Profits), we talk about using "guaranteed delivery" as an effective Give-Get. If a customer decides that they can do without a guaranteed delivery, then they get a lower price. If that customer then calls the president of the company to complain about not getting delivery on time, the president must confirm they lost that guarantee in lieu of the lower price. The goal is that everyone in the organization from the CEO to the delivery people understand that the Give-Gets are operational.

Give-Gets and Inflation

Persistent inflation makes price increases easier to accept. Customers even expect price increases. As long as the demand is strong, you can raise prices. The main requirement is to be agile. By all means, be honest, transparent, and confident in your pricing decisions, but primarily be prepared to move quickly. In this case, time is not your friend. Here are a few ways to safely raise prices in an inflationary market:

- Assign price increases where demand is strong, and your customers' customer will pay for the increase.
- Use Give-Gets to give customers choices instead of a straight price increase. Be proactive and prescriptive in the Give-Gets sellers can apply so pricing does not get compromised. The proper use of the Give-Gets gives your customer a feeling of a partnership during volatile times.
- Raise prices on products that had a low capture rate of differential value. Remember, this means that you are still leaving value on the table for your customers, so don't go over the differential value.
- Concentrate on the markets where the proposed price increase is most insignificant given the overall value of the end solution. In other words, a $100 price change relative to an overall end-user solution of $100,000 (1%) is a lot easier to pass through than a $100 change to a $1,000 end-user solution (10%).
- Raise prices first on customers that consume a high amount of your resources (e.g., high cost to serve) but give you a low return via profitability.
- Modernize governance. This should be in place to avoid cherry-picking bundles and to ensure alignment with strategy and sales tactics.
- Plan adjustments in client contract and renewals to ensure price increases can be put in place when needed.

Good Fences Support Good Give-Gets

When implementing low-value flanking products and value-adding services, product managers express two very real concerns. The first is fear that if they introduce a low-value offering that it will cannibalize demand for their higher-value offerings.

The second concern is that they will not be able to control access to services. If either of these happens, it could wreak havoc with their P&L.

One of the main reasons for having a logical, disciplined offering structure with choices for customers is to prevent them from obtaining high-value offerings for unjustified low prices. Core to any good offering structure is the creation of fences. A fence is just what it sounds like: it prevents customers from getting access to features and services when they haven't paid for them. Product managers can protect value with the right fences.

Recently, we worked with a data provider to help them better understand how customers valued various data and analytic tools. To drive this strategy, the client created a basic platform to enable control of functionality and access to the data. Since most customers initially used the data for screening, this basic functionality was provided to every customer. Customers could add more sophisticated screening techniques by paying more. Functionality, such as adjusting the underlying analysis behind the data, was another add-on. By limiting access to data through functionality and charging specifically for what the client needed, the data provider fenced off high-value functionality, thus protecting the price.

Can your customers see this logic in your offerings? If not, you are eroding their trust. You are also encouraging them to play poker with your sales teams and negotiate more vigorously. If customers don't see logic and integrity in the price-value trade-offs you ask them to make, your business is underperforming relative to its potential. Any measure that you choose to look at—net promoter score, customer longevity, lifetime value, net price realization, average order size—will suffer because of poor fences.

IT distribution is a bloody sport. You have competing manufacturers trying to get your attention, customers who price shop every product they buy, and competitors who will win deals away from you at cost +0.20% margins. How do you sell value in this environment? We worked with one of these distributors to do exactly that. We first found out what customers valued from the distributor. In this case, customers valued their account rep, favorable credit terms, same day delivery, and technical support.

Next, we created three offerings where we varied value drivers enough to create fences for the customers to choose the option they wanted. The first offering was for the price buyer, limiting the customer to transact only over the web at the lowest possible price and have zero access to any services. The second offering gave customers net 30-day terms, discounted tech support fees, and varied delivery based on our priorities. The third offering was the premium offering. Customers in this tier received a dedicated seller, net 60-day terms, guaranteed same day delivery, and free access to technical support for a certain number of calls per month. It took some heavy lifting to implement and train customers to understand these options. The customers appreciated that we made our offerings and fences transparent. We ended up getting over 50 basis points of margin improvement through this transformation. For a 200-basis point business, that's a 25% gain.

Bundling: The Grand Master of Strategic Pricing

A central goal of Give-Gets is to recognize the power of tightening up your offering structure to improve the ability of your sales teams to manage tricky price negotiations. Choices in the offering start with defining the core, then expected, and finally value-added solutions. You're defining low-, medium-, and high-value services, and you are committed to getting paid fairly for them.

There are two challenges that still need to be addressed. The first is the recognition that most businesses sell offerings to different customer segments that recognize varying values for them. The second challenge is within segments, individual customers also value the same offerings differently. Without a well-thought-out plan for managing these two realities, prices will naturally drift downward to accommodate the most price-sensitive customers. Accepting this downward drift is one way to ensure a business is covering its entire market. But it certainly is not the most profitable approach, as it leaves money on the table with those customers that receive high value and are willing to pay more for your offerings.

The way to solve this dilemma is by using bundles. The logic of bundling is straightforward. The idea is to package two or more products, services, or attributes to create variable price-value packages. The benefits include:

1. Creating opportunities to capture more for your value when you have groups of customers that place higher levels of value on the individual components of a potential bundle.

2. Getting customers to buy more than they ordinarily would by offering a financial incentive—a bundled price—that is lower than the sum of the component prices. The key here is to make the savings on the bundle attractive enough that customers will buy the bundle.

Pricing to reach the whole market is the lowest common denominator approach. In contrast, bundling provides a means of getting more revenue from individual elements of the offering than if they were priced to reach the whole market. It allows you to serve all customers while still getting paid more from those customers that place a higher value on your offerings. Let's look at how this works.

Imagine that you are a product manager for a software company providing solutions for tracking customer usage and predicting future behaviors. You are currently focused on the interplay between intercity rail capacity and the desire of casinos to attract gamblers. You've met with a number of customers and gained some great insights.

Casinos place a higher value on the ability to track usage trends of high rollers because it allows them to set triggers to provide complimentary services (comps) in real time, while the high rollers are still on the floor of the casino. The goal, of course, is to keep these high-value customers gambling. The casinos value the ability to predict future spending behaviors of these high rollers so they can cultivate relationships with them.

On the other hand, passenger rail companies are interested in encouraging more people to take the train. With this focus, these companies place more value on use tracking as a means to coordinate simple promotional campaigns. They place some value on trend analysis, but only when they offer collaborative promotions with local hotels.

Figure 8.1 demonstrates the price sensitivity that two types of customers have for two different software products. A gambling casino is willing to pay $600 for the use of tracking software but $1,200 for the trend analysis software since it will help them

	Use Tracking	Trend Analysis
Gambling Casino	$600	$1,200
Passenger Rail Company	$1,000	$400

FIGURE 8.1   Price Sensitivity

determine how to "comp" their loyal customers. The passenger rail company has a higher value ($1,000) for the use tracking software but would only be willing to pay $400 for the trend analysis package. Figure 8.1 shows what the individual prices could be.

Without bundling, if we want to price to cover the whole market, we are forced to the lowest potential prices: $600 for use tracking and $400 for trend analysis. We would then be limited to collecting a maximum of $1,000 for both segments. This leaves a lot of money on the table.

The way out of this predicament is to look at what each segment or use case is willing to pay for both modules together. In this case, casinos are willing to pay $1,800 ($600 for use tracking plus $1,200 for trend analysis). The passenger rail companies are willing to pay a total of $1,400 ($1,000 for use tracking and $400 for trend analysis). By looking at the opportunity this way, we see that we can charge $1,400 for a bundle. This is 40% more. The casino bundle can be priced at $1,800.

The Nuts and Bolts of Bundling

Bundle pricing is an effective strategy under two conditions. First, it's effective when you have multiple complementary products or services to offer. Second, it works when you want to increase the perceived value of low-volume items. When sold together, the complementary products/services offer the customer the most value as well as improve their purchasing experience.

Given how critical bundling is to the financial health of your organization, we need to spend more time laying the groundwork for lining up the objectives. A credible set of bundles is the result of following a straightforward process. First, start with a simple approach to customer segments. In Rule Four (Know Your Value), we described the customer triggers of value. Going back to the data provider example, they knew its data was of high value. It was selling tens of millions of dollars' worth of information products every year.

What the company didn't know was how customers were actually using the data in their investment decision-making process. Customer interviews uncovered three different uses for the data. The majority of customers applied their own analytic processes to scroll down the universe of potential investments to select a reasonable subset for easier investing decisions. Some customers wanted to alter the assumptions behind the data to create new portfolios for their own analysis. Still other customers used the data as a reality check against analysis and decisions their own advisors had performed—in other words, a risk mitigation technique. Effective bundles can be a competitive advantage that will draw in demand from competitors. This simple understanding of customer use cases provided the basis for the following insights:

- Bundling products and services works in almost every buying environment. It simplifies the purchase and causes customers to buy more because of the discount of the bundle versus the individual prices of items. The discount doesn't need to be large—something on the order of 10 to 15% can be effective.

- To work, bundle prices should be lower than the combined prices of the components. If the price of any of the individual items in the bundle is significantly lower, the incentive to buy the bundle is lost. You can't use a bundle to raise the prices of the components unless you raise the component prices too! If you can't control the prices of your components, bundles won't solve the problems either.

- Individual product prices continually are rationalized with the prices of all bundles in which they are included, even during promotions. That is the way you protect the integrity of the bundle—buyers need to know they are getting the best deal in the bundle.

- Developing Give-Gets options within a bundle is one of the most powerful sales tools account managers can use to execute more profitable deals.

The lessons here can apply to all companies that offer bundled or packaged solutions for customers. Right now, we are seeing a lot of interest by clients who want to start bundling to try to make up for declining sales due to the COVID-19 pandemic. Recognize first that declining demand isn't solved by a bundle.

Don't Bungle the Bundle!

Bundling of products and services works. It simplifies the purchase and encourages customers to buy more products or services. To reiterate, the bundled price must be lower than the combined prices of the components. Once the price of any of the individual products gets to a certain level, there is no incentive to buy the bundle. Individual product prices require regular maintenance and comparison with the prices of all bundles in which they are included, even those for short-term promotions. This way, you protect the integrity of the bundle.

If you adopt lower prices for the individual components, your customers will be able to break the bundle and buy individual components for a lower total price. In addition to allowing the prices of the individual components of the bundle to be too low, there are two other ways that managers typically "bungle the bundle."

Allowing customers to break the bundle during price negotiations destroys price integrity. A supplier of industrial components offered discounts based on the number of items on an order and total dollar volume: a legitimate form of bundling for large accounts. Poker-playing customers tried to cherry-pick the individual items that appear to have the best individual prices from the supplier and give the rest of the business to competitors.

Companies do this out of fear of losing all of the business. The end result was that the incentives used to encourage placing the entire order with this supplier were gutted and street prices on the individual items fell precipitously. Over time, this fear caused the company to be sold to a competitor.

A better way is to show percentage discounts for the total piece of business and not let the customer place orders with the lower prices. The discounts should have been earned and granted after the volume met the required levels.

McDonald's is at the heart of our favorite bungle the bundle stories. McDonald's once offered a 10% discount to drive demand for French fries. This caused a drop in combo meals and resulted in more sales of the 99-cent burger. The combo meals are a traditional winner for franchises as customers who normally buy just the burger and a drink opt to add fries at a discount. Customers might even justify "supersizing" their order given the "bargain" the bundling represents. McDonald's dollar promotions were successful as far as selling hamburgers went but short-circuited the purchases of combo deals, which had been a solid mainstay of the product offering for the chain.

The bundling strategy leads to greater customer satisfaction, higher sales, and higher profits. But like everything else with price strategy, bundling needs to be executed with precision. If a great marketing company like McDonald's can "bungle their bundle," well, you get the rest.

"Never confuse motion with action," Benjamin Franklin warned the business leaders of Colonial America. We doubt Franklin ever got into price competition when he sold subscriptions to Poor Richard's Almanack, the publication Franklin produced from 1732 to 1758. But he was way ahead of us on pricing strategy. He used fences and Give-Gets such as differing levels of subscriptions and tactics such as serialization so that readers would purchase the almanac year after year to find out what happened to the characters described in the preceding almanac. Franklin delivered value and priced the almanac accordingly. He retired at age 42 off the proceeds.

CHAPTER 9

Rule Nine

Build Your Selling Backbone

You can't capture any price until you have Selling Backbone. We use "Backbone" to mean "something which resists bending." Even the best price strategy will fail unless salespeople, managers, and senior leaders demonstrate backbone in the selling and negotiating process. Backbone is the "last mile of pricing—the people closest to the customer—the sales force, the commercial team, and the leadership that directs them. Without backbone in the price execution process, firms are condemned to leaving money on the table.

We start with a story that explains every wrinkle of Building Your Selling Backbone. The call came from one of our largest clients. The EVP of sales requested our help in a delicate sales negotiation with a customer they couldn't afford to lose. He wanted our counsel to price the solution, knowing upcoming negotiations with one of its largest customers would be nail-biting. It helped our client capture its largest and most profitable customer.

Some background: The company was a semiconductor manufacturer with a handful of large global competitors that offered related products The products were a mature commodity in a highly price-sensitive market. We understood that their customer—a well-known maker of disk drives—required a growing volume of semiconductors to support drive assembly and the imminent release of a new product.

The first step was to embark on a value hunt. A value hunt is a process to how the selling company adds value and differentiates its feature set. This forms the foundation for establishing a fair price. Our goal was to determine exactly what features the disk drive manufacturer required to pinpoint value. Our client sent a team of trained technicians to visit the disk drive maker's design team. The scouting team came back with a five-page list of technical features that the disk drive manufacturer desired. Yet, there were no incremental value opportunities in the list. The specified semiconductors in the deal were commodities; all the competitors offered the same set of specifications.

We needed information we could use to differentiate our client's product from the competitors. We tried to set up additional formal meetings with customer's technicians and the design team responsible for building the next-generation disk drives. At this point, the customer's purchasing agent became an obstacle, insisting on controlling the relationship and denying interviews.

Every obstacle yields to an elegant solution. In this case, when formality failed, we tried informality. At lunchtime, we had our team stop by the customer's offices carrying hot pizza and cold soft drinks. The technicians were invited in, and conversations ensued. They were able to piece together some intelligence that would prove to be valuable.

Two Preferred Vendors

First, we learned that of the eight potential vendors, the disk drive company really preferred two vendors. One of the preferred vendors was the client we represented, and the other was its largest competitor. Second, we learned that the customer had critical delivery requirements to meet the expected demand for their new drives. These two facts were quite favorable for our client because it had an excellent history for meeting delivery requirements that were better than the competition. Now we could get to work devising a specific price strategy.

We calculated that the incremental value derived by the disk drive customer from choosing our client's semiconductors rather than the competitors came down to four dollars per unit. We had to make sure their pricing met the fairness test. There was a lot of discussion around what percentage of the incremental four dollars per unit of value our client could requisition and still be fair to the customer.

In the end, we advised our client to charge an extra 25%, or an additional one dollar per unit. We argued that the increase of one dollar was a fair exchange for the four dollars per unit of incremental value. We understood that the competitor would most likely charge at least one dollar less, and that the procurement person would use aggressive poker-playing tactics to get our client to lower their price.

The Negotiations Ensue

The first step in any negotiation is to know your opponent's position better than they do. Based on our insights, we predicted the moves the customer made. First, the customer's purchasing agent argued, threatened, and bluffed our client's selling team. Fortunately, we had prepared the team to defend themselves. The prescribed language: "We'll be pleased to meet the lower price, but at that price we cannot give you the delivery guarantees you expect."

The customer's purchasing agent upped the game playing. He cancelled meetings at the last minute. He made our client's pricing team cool their heels. He telephoned our client's executives attempting to exploit weaknesses in the pricing strategy.

Having been trained in a new level of selling backbone, our client's selling team anticipated all his moves and wouldn't budge. Eventually, the purchasing agent caved.

Like every good negotiation, it turned out to be a win-win. In subsequent years, the customer sold 13 million disk drives incorporating our client's semiconductors. The disk drive customer became our client's most profitable customer overnight. By going on a value hunt and with prepared negotiation plans, our client grabbed an additional $12.5 million off the table.

The Key Elements of Backbone

For Backbone to work, sellers need to ask two simple questions.

The first question uncovers the true buying behavior of the customer. Customers have different agendas for different vendors. Each agenda and subsequent buyer behavior requires a vendor to prepare different offerings or solutions, pricing, selling, and negotiating approaches. There are four types of buyers that represent observable behaviors around the world. Understanding those behaviors helps a seller craft a more efficient and profitable approach to the customer before, during, and after a negotiation. Let's introduce the four groups.

Price Buyers. These customers buy exclusively on price. They don't care about value-added enhancements, nor do they care about fancy bells and whistles. They establish purchasing criteria for a wide range of possible vendors and make sure they qualify everyone to bid on the business. Price buyers are careful not to let themselves commit to any particular supplier and make sure they have no switching costs. You can tell a price buyer primarily because they are frequently switching vendors in pursuit of the lowest possible price. If you want to sell to a price buyer at a profit, you need to have the lowest possible cost.

Value Buyers. Value buyers have recognized the flaws of purchasing based on price and have extremely sophisticated technical or business process people who regularly evaluate the value that alternative vendors offer. Their goal is to quantify that value and choose the best of the alternatives from a limited set of trusted vendors. Value buyers are fairly upfront about what their agenda is. It's important in approaching a value buyer that you first need to understand the value they are looking for, showing them along the way that you can be or already are a trustworthy vendor.

Relationship Buyers. Relationship buyers rely on close relationships with trusted suppliers to meet their needs. As a general rule, relationship buyers already have relationships with a particular trusted vendor in each area. They will, on occasion, realize that the current vendor can no longer meet their needs. At that point, they will often move to value buying behavior to evaluate a small group of trusted vendors. If a seller is one of those trusted vendors, they need to stay ahead of the evolving needs of this particular customer, always looking for new ways to meet their needs. If you are on the outside, you need to have endless patience. Patience to show that you are trustworthy, in many cases without getting any business from the client. It can happen by meeting small customer needs to show that you can be a trusted vendor. The trick is to stay close to the customer so that when they have a need the current vendor can't meet, they will come to you.

Poker Players. Poker players are value and relationship buyers who have learned that if they focus on price, they can often get vendors to discount high-value features and services. Poker players have learned that desperate suppliers will do just about anything to get their business. The key to identifying poker players is determining whether they are really value buyers or relationship buyers disguised as a price buyer.

The first modern book on value, *Techniques of Value Analysis and Engineering*, focused on how to get lower costs from suppliers. It was the first step in educating procurement people to become poker players. Written by Lawrence D. Miles, a former procurement professional for General Electric, the book argued and advocated that businesses engage professional training for procurement people to expertly negotiate lower prices. Since then, most countries have professional associations of procurement people that do extensive training on how to play poker with vendors.

Interestingly, many companies overestimate the ratio of price buyers to value and relationship buyers. On average, professional sellers estimate that 70% of their customers are price buyers. Our research determined that, in fact, only 30% of customers were price buyers. The difference of 40% is made up of the poker players. We believe that number is growing dramatically in a wide range of industries around the world.

Buyer Behaviors and Inflation

In inflationary markets, sellers are assigned to present price increases. This is an uncomfortable job in the best of times and more difficult when customers feel the weight of costs rising. How do you prepare your sales teams to deliver the price increase message and get it to stick? First, regardless of the buyer's behavior, prepare for customer objections. A whiteboard exercise with the commercial team will highlight most objections and allow them to thoughtfully prepare answers.

- For price buyers, give them the option to accept the increase. In the alternative, void the contract. If you have constrained capacity or supply chain interruptions, it is better that available products go to high-value customers first.

- Value buyers need choices. While discussing the increase on their current product, offer a lower value option. This will improve your overall customer relationship because they see you have their best interests at heart.
- Relationship buyers will best understand the need for the price increase. Importantly for this group, don't gouge them relative to other buyer types. This is a sure way to lose trust and long-term commitment.
- Poker players (value or relationship buyers in disguise) will push back the hardest on the increase. First, expose their true behavior. You might do this by offering to cancel the current contract. That will get a reaction. Then discuss an increase or a lower value option.

The most crucial element in implementing a price increase is that all customers take the increase. Otherwise, you later alienate the customers that took the increase, realizing that others did not. This creates more poker-playing customers.

Your Position at the Table

The second question uncovers what your true relationship with the decision maker is and how that positions you at the table. Think about whether you as the seller have a positive relationship with the decision maker. Indifference on the part of the customer means you lack a positive relationship. You must not allow yourself to be deceived on this point.

What's a good relationship? It starts with open and honest discussions with the decision-maker. It means they will honestly tell you where you stand and how you can help them better serve their customers. They will be forthcoming with criticism as well as praise. Both are gifts. Decision makers are budget owners, rarely procurement people. As a general rule, the only time procurement people are decision makers is when they are price buyers. All other times, they're just playing poker and they are experts at bluffing you.

Several years ago, we were working with a large paper company. We received a call from a senior sales executive who wanted our advice while preparing for a high-stakes negotiation. Their strategy was perfect for a relationship buyer. Unfortunately, we determined that the customer was truly a price buyer. After discussions, we predicted that her company had little chance of winning the business from this particular buyer using the indicated strategy. We suggested the executive change her strategy or use her time to focus on more promising customers. The executive angrily rejected our recommendation and plowed ahead with her team to prepare for the battle. Two weeks later they lost the deal.

How did we know the buyer in question was a price buyer and not a relationship buyer as the executive assumed? At one time, our client did enjoy a long-term relationship with the customer. But the customer had recently been acquired by a conglomerate that had a long history of price buying. Further, we learned that the buyer from the conglomerate had taken over the purchasing of the particular product offered and had invited a large number of other companies to submit bids along with our client's. This was clearly a price buying situation.

Backbone requires a clear understanding of the facts and preparation. To win in the game of customer negotiations, the salesperson and executives must have an unobstructed vision of what it is the customer genuinely wants, what they're willing to pay, and the ability to subsequently deliver. Understanding the customer's likely buying behavior is critical because it tells the seller, first, whether there is a chance of winning the business and, second, what needs to be done to make sure no money is left on the table. Your position at the table tells you whether you have a real chance of winning the business.

RFPs – Learning Not to Dance with the Devil

At this point, it's worthwhile to spend a few moments talking about Requests for Proposal (RFPs). An RFP or tender is often a signal that a customer is trying to do one of four things. First, they are using the tactic to drive down the price of the incumbent vendor. Second, they are on a fishing expedition to see how a wide range of vendors will respond and have no immediate need. Third, they are a value buyer putting a limited number of vendors through their paces or, fourth, they are a true price buyer. Knowing the correct reason for the RFP will help you decide whether you should even bid and, if you do, whether you have a chance of winning the bid and making a profit. If you don't know the reason, don't respond until you do know the reason.

Before we give you any prescription, please answer the following questions.

- What percentage of your RFPs do you win?
- How much time do your people spend on responding to each RFP?

With respect to the first question, we are constantly surprised that our clients do not have the data to answer this simple question. With respect to the second, if you are dedicating more than a few hours of staff time to the average RFP and your close rate is below 20%, you are probably wasting resources responding to RFPs.

It's a sad fact that dominant vendors to an account respond to customer RFPs too often. This is especially true when the RFP indicates a shift in buying responsibility from a technical person or a user to the purchasing agent. This is also the case when there is a third-party consultant managing the bid process. The worst thing that a dominant incumbent can do is to respond to the RFP. When they do, they are either going to have to drop their price significantly to win the business they already enjoy or they are looking at losing the bid to a low-value vendor. Selling with backbone is a much better way of dealing with this tactic than responding to RFPs. Let us tell you a story about a firm that didn't cut off a customer's attempt at running an RFP with a few simple words.

We encountered a situation with a financial services client that was the preferred vendor for a $10 million bank audit contract that had to be done quickly. The customer bank hired a large consulting firm to manage the negotiation, a clear indication that they were playing poker. We believed that the consulting firm would justify its fee by telling the bank that it would be successful in getting our client to reduce prices dramatically. Because we were prepared, our selling with backbone discipline devastated the consulting firm's strategy.

Our client's partner made her presentation to the bank, quickly closed up her computer, and started leaving the room. The poker playing consultant stopped her and said they might put the job out to bid. The partner then said, "We thought you might do that. If you do, our price will go up, and we won't be able to do the job in the time you need." Then she quickly left the room. We had fun picturing the bank executives hammering the poker-playing consultant. Our client closed the deal at $10 million few days later.

The Importance of Trust

In dealing with both relationship and value buyers, trust is vital. Research we conducted found that there were two major drivers of price buying behavior. The first driver was the size of the company. Larger companies have the wherewithal to develop the internal expertise they need to create extensive specifications and evaluate alternative vendors based on their ability to meet those specifications. But even large firms rely on trusted vendors in areas of professional services and advanced technologies.

The second driver was the level of trust in both the selling company and the salesperson. That's important because if there isn't a plan to develop trust with customers, they are going to be either price buyers or poker players.

We recently had a conversation with the CEO of a large technology company. The CEO was building a home, and we were a reference for a builder he was considering using. The CEO said the main requirement was that the builder would be on time and come in on budget. The goals were reasonable. Then we told him about someone who had the same objectives. That person found a builder that delivered the construction on time and on budget. But in year one, the homeowner had to replace all the cabinets and the floors in the house. Why? Because most builders can give you a house on time and on budget if they cut corners. And they will have to cut corners because the nature of building a significant home is inherently unpredictable. Much more important than empty promises, we suggested, is trust.

This CEO accepted the wisdom of what we said. What he really wanted in a builder was someone trustworthy to deal with the unpredictable nature of building a home the CEO would be happy with. As much as the CEO traveled, he had to depend on the builder for making day-to-day decisions, some of which were bound to impact schedule and budget. We recounted our positive experience with this builder: how we did work without contracts, with flexible budgets, and all on a handshake. Maybe you think we are foolish. But we can tell you that when you trust someone with expertise and integrity, the work is usually better. Plus the experience is more enjoyable.

Many companies still prefer to deal with vendors they trust. They save a lot of worry and money overall and get high-quality results each and every time. We have a true trusting relationship with one of our largest clients. We work as if we are true employees, and they trust us to do the right thing. We can be open and honest with them and are willing to make deep commitments to their success. Believe us, it's a wonderful way to do business.

Create High-Impact Value Messages and Sales Tools

Documenting value is an important way to justify prices and define offerings and is not persuasive. If sales professionals can't defend the logic behind different offering and pricing options, then they will be in an uncomfortable position when they present to customers. The solution is to give the sales professionals the tools that they need to sell value and defend prices.

To do this, the sales professionals must be able to put customer value discoveries to further use. These discoveries need to be put into a simple model to show how customers derive measurable value from the company's various offerings. This segmentation provides a structure of questions for customers to help the sales team determine how their products and services financially impact the customer's business on a case-by-case basis.

Unfortunately, most ROI tools that marketers provide to salespeople don't work. The major reason they fail is that salespeople find them too complicated or not believable and therefore don't use them. Another reason is that a sizable number of customers who go to the trouble of doing the analysis don't trust the results.

The solution is to develop sales tools that use the customer's own data. The analysis should provide explicit consideration of competitive alternatives. The objective is to make the customer's purchasing decision easier, not harder, by hiding information from them. Presenting data that gives direct visibility to your competition can seem counterintuitive to many sales professionals. Why invite comparison that might strengthen the customer's negotiating position? The fact is that comparing your products with those of competitors highlights both strengths and weaknesses. Balanced selling actually improves the credibility of salespeople.

In addition to issues of credibility, there is another major difference. Traditional ROI modeling often provides data on the average customer, aggregated at some level for a group of customers. Detailed comparison is left in the hands of the customer, who may not judge accurately or fairly. Providing a case-by-case comparison ensures that sellers remain involved during the evaluation process by providing all needed details. With this approach, customers are more likely to trust the data.

Credible sales tools are easy to construct. If customers cannot get comparative data directly from potential suppliers, they will develop their own internal models to facilitate comparison. Once they have done so, they will rarely share the full details of their analysis. Instead, they will use the information to pit one vendor against another in a game of price negotiation.

Backbone During Inflation

Selling Backbone is even more critical during inflationary times. It's perhaps more important now than ever before because procurement people are upping their game to secure lower prices. Fortunately, they are also admitting to a critical weakness that you need to know about so you can bluff them at the poker table. How do we know? Because we listen to procurement podcasts to find out what they're up to.

Procurement will resist your argument that inflation merits cost increases. Throughout this book, we've talked about the need to increase prices because your costs are going up. To do that, you've got to prepare your sales teams to execute those increase with Backbone. Why? Because the procurement people are already preparing their responses to your sales teams. They are loading up on responses such as, "No, we don't have the budget, you'll have to absorb the cost increase yourself." Another common maneuver is stall techniques: Break down the cost to explain the increase.

The critical weakness for many customers is their need for reliability of supply. From commodities to high-value professional services around the world, procurement people understand that in these turbulent times, reliable supply is often a problem. Remember, their primary job is to ensure a supply of quality products and services to keep their own business humming without interruption. Interruption is extremely costly. You can use that certainty in your negotiating to blunt their poker-playing ways. How? Use reliability of supply as an expression of Give-Gets. If the buyer refuses to accept your price increase, respond that they can either accept the increase or you can no longer assure them of a reliable supply. This works every time.

Procurement people know that this is unchartered territory for vendors they face across the negotiating table. They know you don't know how to raise prices with a contract in place. They know you are focusing on maintaining the relationship and want to know how serious you are. Backbone is the "serious" they are looking for. We'll talk about this in Rule Ten (Deploy Three Practices to Increase Profits).

Vishal Kumar is president of AmeCast in New Delhi, India. The company specializes in replacement cast parts in stainless steel and high alloys for domestic industrial plants and the process industry. The executive teams have been using Backbone for over 10 years. Due to the latest downturn in demand and inflation, the company developed a price/value matrix for all of their products. To sort out the serious buyers, all inquiries get referred to the company's website, which has extensive information. The company expects serious buyers to qualify themselves before the company invests considerable effort. In addition, the company captures the value it offers by charging for all value-added services, such as visiting a customer's manufacturing facilities. To deal with price competition from lower quality Chinese competitors, AmeCast reliably applies Give-Gets. For example, Vishal was entertained by a large company that was attempting to make him pay a fee to submit a bid. The demand for the initial fee was 500 Indian Rupees (about \$6.45). When Vishal told them he wouldn't pay anything, the company dropped the request to 100 Rupees (about \$1.29). Desperate times bring out the worst in buyers, especially when they push to nickel and dime you, but having Backbone mitigates the pain and, at least in this case, gives our clients permission to have fun with unreasonable buyers.

Critical Elements of Selling Backbone

There are a few key elements for companies that want to see the benefits of increased revenue and profits from Selling with Backbone:

- **Get senior executive support** Senior executives need to learn, embrace, and support Backbone. Senior executives who understand the value of your firm will support efforts to charge fair and consistent prices in the marketplace.

- **Target the right customers with the right deals.** Not all customers can be good customers: good to deal with and growing profitably. Price buyers need to be profitable, or you need a path to profitability before you close the deal. Conversely, good poker playing identifies the value and relationship buyers in price buyer clothing and does the necessary things to keep your prices where they should be.

- **Embrace value at your core as an individual and firm.** This is not just paying lip service to the term "value." We are talking about putting value at the core of a corporate culture and organizational belief system. We are fortunate to collaborate with a company president who embraces value. When this executive takes leadership of a division, it may take a year or more to sort through the opportunity, but he improves the division by believing in its value and expecting his people to do the same. In a recent training session, one sales rep suddenly realized that her largest customer was playing poker with her. With her new-found Selling Backbone, the sales rep went back to the negotiating table, demonstrated how her products specifically were saving that client millions of dollars. She and her team negotiated an additional $3 million profit on $80 million worth of business.

The bottom line of this discussion is that you can't implement fair pricing unless you have Selling Backbone. Irrespective of product, service, industry, and geographic location, pricing with confidence is all about Selling with Backbone.

CHAPTER 10

Rule Ten

Deploy Three Practices to Increase Profits

Price theory and complex models are great but success in pricing often comes from a few practices we've learned over the years to dramatically improve profits. These practices, straightforward and easy to communicate, make these practices easy to implement even in complex organizations challenged by the highest sustained inflation rates in four decades.

What is the foremost goal of a successful business? To serve customers at a profit. Without the profit part, you don't have a business but a hobby. Now, the profit part may seem obvious, but you'd be surprised how often in the midst of intense price competition, the profit imperative is missing in action. We've seen profitability take a rear seat in so many negotiations across all industries and verticals. No business is immune. Repeatedly, we've seen our clients become so mired in details and day-to-day fire drills that they lose focus on the profit prize.

Our ultimate advice is to focus on profit first. Do that well, and you'll spend less time worrying about revenue and volume.

This truth is doubly true when considering price strategy in inflationary times. But know this: there is no magic silver bullet to "fix" inflation with pricing. The goal is to maintain profitability and work to grow in an inflationary market. We must carefully manage the levers in our control and pull them at the right time, for the right reasons, and at the right places (i.e., strategic implementation).

Importantly, pricing professionals should not roll out an average broad stroke price increase across the board. Have a thoughtful plan to raise prices where demand is strong, and customers feel there is value. Build your organization for speed. Start by modernizing governance to ensure increases stick. In volatile markets, conditions can change rapidly. Today it's about inflation, tomorrow it may be something else. Have the right plan and process to get ahead of whatever may come next.

Maintaining Profitability During Inflation

It's no secret that the world is dealing with the worst inflation in four decades. Globally, inflation is cutting into the profits of companies in every industry. Businesses across the world are scrambling to deal with the dramatic increases in costs along with supply chain problems and labor shortages arising from the global COVID-19 pandemic.

Inflation makes sellers feel that it upends every aspect to defending their value proposition. The good news is that businesses can flourish even during inflation. Yes, it's inevitable that companies will have to raise prices. But increasing prices should be thoughtful and products should be chosen with surgical precision.

Customers are unique. Instead of instituting across-the-board price increases, deploy fine-tuned increases informed by the value received by the customer, cost to serve, and historical performance. Don't be afraid to walk away from low-value customers who resist the price increase. In this case it's critical to support your sales professionals when walking away is the right choice. Your efforts should be to replace the loss of a low-value customers with a customer more attractive to your bottom line.

- Consider charging for indirect increases. Besides direct price increases tied to inflation indexes, B2B companies can pass on surcharges for fuel, expedited shipping, inventory holding, and longer payment terms. Challenge low-value customers that leak profits with such practices as rush orders, partial truck deliveries, delayed terms, etc. If they won't pay the fees, let them go elsewhere.
- Swap price for other valuable features. Prepare for customers resisting a straight increase, by offering other benefits. These range from supply volume guarantees to bundled products or adjusted service levels.
- Take care to enforce terms that are already in the customer contract. Review and enforce the contingencies for price increases that may exist. Equip sales professionals with the data and scripts to have any expected difficult conversations with backbone. The average industrial company loses over 6% of revenue through off-invoice discounts and leakage, according to a global sample analyzed by Bain and Price. That's a nice bucket of profits to grab back.
- Adjust the product mix. During a period of inflation and supply shocks, it's critical to have an up-to-the-minute SKU-level view of profitability. Just as it sometimes makes sense to walk away from low-value customers, companies may be obliged to drop marginally profitable products and services.

Hedge Now

Prepare your organization now to hedge against a medium or long-term inflation scenario. Most corporate leaders have not dealt with macro inflation during their careers, leaving them unsure of how to proceed. Organizations dedicated to taking pricing steps grounded with Selling Backbone need to assess their inflation exposure. Typically, the finance team leads an exercise that reveals baseline details of how profits would shift under different inflation scenarios. In granular detail, the analysis considers which products and services contribute to profitability and which customers can be served at a profit.

Such a baseline establishes the organization and sets it on a path with strong footing to undertake the optimal pricing actions. Rather than trying to solve the entire problem at once, it pays to sequence which customers and distribution channels to tackle first. Set priorities based on customer profitability or contract renewal dates. Using a customized pricing plan and ensuring salespeople are confident leadership will support them making the tough decisions needed with different customers. This will allow organizations to improve their competitive position during a heavy inflation market, plus build the capability to adjust prices quickly whenever it's warranted.

It's understandable that B2B companies may be reluctant to do what's necessary to protect profits during inflationary times. Many companies granted their customers pricing relief due to the pandemic, and now they are sunk into a pricing hole and inflation is devouring profits. Fixing this problem requires having difficult conversations. It might involve breaking informal arrangements with channel partners and customers. It's difficult to tell good customers that they are facing longer waits for products and higher prices. Yet inflationary conditions favor organizations that act swiftly to implement responsive price strategies.

The good news, if there is any, is that if customer leaders think it's fair, even if painful, they will absorb or pass on price increases due to inflation. These customers will not, however, give their suppliers much credit for delaying price increases only to push them through 6 or 12 months from now. For supply-constrained industries, customers have limited alternatives with which to negotiate. Price could very well be less important than supply and inventory availability.

Here's an example of how one company dealt with inflation.

For a regional car service company, the pandemic years had been tough on their company's business. Many of the company's best customers had stopped business travel in favor of conducting business via videoconferencing. The company ended up selling some of its vehicles. When that wasn't enough, it was forced to furlough drivers. As the pandemic gave way to more travel, the company was further shocked by inflation in the form of dramatically rising fuel costs. The owner had no choice but to raise fares. We listened sympathetically as the owner talked about how he had so many loyal customers and that he was reluctant to see a price increase damage the personal relationships he had with them.

Here's what we told him. Pricing in inflationary times is a lot like playing musical chairs. When the first competitor raises prices, they might lose a little business, but most competitors will follow quickly. If you wait too long to increase prices, worrying about your loyal customers, you are soon going to be inundated by new customers who are price buyers. These customers will be glad to take advantage of your cheaper car service. The results are predictable. These marginally profitable and fickle customers will overload and impact the quality of service expected by loyal, existing customers. No one wins in that scenario.

Honest reflection during inflationary times will allow business leaders to recognize that costs are going up, and therefore prices must rise as well. Realize that your loyal customers already know this. The value buyers will probably stick around. The price buyers might leave for a while, but they are the most likely to be unprofitable, so it might be a blessing in disguise to see them go.

Business is about earning a reasonable return for the value your company delivers. Profitability becomes the lifeblood of companies if they can address these three practices.

Practice One: Know Which Pricing Approach to Employ

Imagine a sales conversation unfolding like this.

SALESPERSON:	"So, you're interested?"
POTENTIAL CUSTOMER:	"You know, we might be. How much will it cost us?"
SALESPERSON	"That depends—let's see which features and options are right for you."

Notice what's happening here. The salesperson is setting up the conversation for profit-based pricing. The first imperative of any business facing a sales negotiation is to understand value. This pricing approach is used by businesses who are confident that they can provide solutions that produce measurable benefits for the customer. The key is to engage with the customer's perceived value of the product or service in question. Profit pricing is customer-focused pricing. In more technical terms, it's a method of setting a price that allows a business to calculate and earn the differentiated worth of its product for a particular customer segment when compared to its competitor.

Many organizations take an "inside-out" approach to pricing, and price to cover costs. This can often lead to missed opportunities or pricing that's too high. Others set prices to meet market conditions or to drive market share. Unfortunately, when done incorrectly, this approach can lead to leaving money on the table, or worse, starting a price war.

Profit-based pricing is an "outside-in" approach to pricing. Combined with basic and complex analytics, it will deliver price improvements and price points tied to differential value. Companies who employ this approach to pricing can drive profitable growth because the organization can:

- Set price levels with confidence to create a clear rationale for pricing.
- Articulate the differentiated P&L impact of your offering to your customer.
- Align cross-functionally to understand, create, and monetize value for sustainable results.
- Focus on mutually beneficial growth by creating stronger relationships with customers.

Remember, value, as always, is determined by the customer.

The CEO of a technology startup that manufactured ceramic circuit boards approached us with a problem. The CEO (let's call him Barry) shared how hard it was to move beyond a large client that was extracting price concession after price concession. His company was losing money on this client. We offered to send a consultant over to guide the client's sales team to figure out the answer to that question and suggest some potential remedies.

A little background: The company supplied circuit boards for a supplier to the U.S. Navy. The circuit boards proved successful in the radar system in the nose cones of F-18 Hornets fighter jets. The six circuit boards aboard each Hornet were 400 pounds lighter than the older version.

It quickly became clear to us that the company had a superpower. The ceramic circuit boards it supplied to the U.S. Navy were unmatched by any competitor in a number of technical specifications. The boards were lighter, more reliable, and could operate in higher heat conditions than the competition. The company by and large didn't understand what a huge competitive advantage this conferred. When the consultant delivered her report, the value to the customer of the company's circuit boards came into sharp and indisputable relief. Such knowledge is power. That gets us to the second part of UVPF: Price Fair. The buyer may grimace at the price but will eventually come to agree that given the value the product delivers, it is fair.

Fairness Is Critical

The concept of fairness is critical. Both sides must agree to the essential fairness of the price. Everyone understands fair pricing. The procurement people may not want to admit it, but they know their vendors need a fair profit or the relationship they often come to depend on will be unsustainable. It's never in a customer's interest to bankrupt a vendor they depend on. A fair price is one that, given your costs, similar competitive products, and a reasonable share of the incremental value the products generate, the stakeholders agree is fair.

Some analysts argue that a price that captures 25% of incremental value is fair. We disagree. Sometimes the fair number is just 5%. There are times when fairness is capturing 50%. It's all based on the situation, the competition, the nature of the current relationship, and the relationship you desire for the future.

Fairness may be more art than science. We recently did some work in financial services where the product was priced at $22. The primary research showed that customers would not resist a 7 to 8% price increase. That's not bad, but a look at the value the product generated revealed that the client benefited to the tune of $60 per sale. The sales team decided to lead with a price increase of $50. After some internal back and forth, the parties agreed to a price increase of $48. A satisfied customer and certainly more profitable for the financial services firm was the result.

Here's another example of value-based pricing using the UVPF (Understand Value, Price Fairly) formula.

We collaborated with a company whose sales team was convinced their product was a commodity. The assumption reinforced that there was no choice but to reduce price to remain competitive. We went to work to surface reasons why the product was a trade good with unique value. Interviews with customers and decision makers supported our view. Further analysis demonstrated that while the product indeed functioned as a commodity, our client was the preferred vendor in most cases. This was because among the competitors, there were wide variations in product quality, reliability of supply, and customer service.

The company's products were really a staple rather than a commodity and were essential for their customers. The company decided there was over-supply and announced it was taking one of its manufacturing plants off-line. That step alarmed the customers because they knew that when supply goes down and demand stays the same, prices go up. In fact, the sales team announced that prices were, indeed, to be raised. The sales team said they would honor existing prices for customers who put in orders immediately. Some customers thought it a bluff and that prices would be maintained. We acknowledge even some of the client's own salespeople didn't believe the strategy would work and customers would rebel.

In fact, when the company followed through with the announced price increase, customers left in droves. It was a tense situation for a few weeks. Some customers tried a competitor but found that it could not reliably satisfy demand. Other competitors took the opportunity to match our client's price increase. In the following weeks, one customer after another decided it was in their interest to accept the price increase for the more reliable supply and superior customer service. This company discovered that all their customers were poker players. That's why UVPF is so important.

Practice Two: Play Better Poker

The poker player is the hardest customer to deal with. These are the buyers disguised as price buyers who want high value for low price and are accustomed to getting it. They negotiate for the lowest prices and burn through increased services. Professional Procurement Organizations have been offering certification programs around the world to teach their members how to better play the game. If you want to stop leaving money on the table when you are negotiating with poker players, you simply have to play better poker or not play at all.

There are a number of reasons that customers play poker. One is that they have learned not to trust their vendors. The biggest reason, however, is because experience shows them it just works. Most vendors, large and small, in very high value markets, just don't know how to effectively respond to poker players. There are only three ways to win at poker: have a winning hand, bluff, or fold. Most successful poker-playing customers don't want to rely on the luck of the draw, and they generally prefer not to drive away vendors with whom they have a successful relationship. But they are very eager to bluff. This is what many purchasing agents have specialized in over the years. The problem is that salespeople and their managers can't match their skill. Nor do they realize the strength of their own hand. Without the confidence in their solutions, salespeople and managers lose in customer negotiations because they are desperate to close the deal and will do so at any price.

Several years ago we were introduced to Michael, the president of a small company that sold competitive intelligence to government contractors. The product was clearly high-value knowledge, but he was endlessly getting beat up on price by the clients' procurement professionals. What did he do? He learned to play better poker. He quickly understood what was needed and started pricing the value services higher and having a low-value flanking product as a Give-Get for the negotiation. The results were a dramatic increase in both revenue and profitability.

Learning to use price to control capacity utilization is the ultimate control mechanism to maximize profits and revenue at the same time. The trick is not to overcomplicate it as many organizations have done to their detriment. The goal is to keep it simple, have everyone in the organization understand what it is, and why it is important. Then empower everyone up and down the line to do what they need to do in order to focus the company on profitability.

Practice Three: Better Leverage Resources

In 2006, Amazon Web Services (AWS) began offering IT infrastructure services to businesses in the form of web services— now commonly known as cloud computing. AWS understood the three absolute levers of value that customers would be quick to recognize. First, customers would perceive immediate value in having access to an array of cloud computing services without the need for up-front capital infrastructure expenses. Second, customers would see immediately the benefit in the ability to access the services with low variable costs that scale as the customer's needs increase or decrease. Third, how much value would customers assign to getting productive almost immediately? No longer would they have to plan for and procure IT infrastructure weeks or months in advance. Would any customer not see the value of being able to instantly spin up hundreds or thousands of servers in minutes and deliver results to their own customers faster?

In 2009, AWS made a radical change to its pricing model. It switched from the standard subscription pay-for-what-you-deploy pricing model to the untested risky events-based billing approach. It was risky for AWS. How could any company plan for and meet quarterly revenue goals with such a volatile and unpredictable pricing model?

But AWS had done its homework. AWS understood the market. Most of all it knew what its customers required, even if the customers themselves were not yet quite aware of it. The analytics it generated persuaded AWS leaders that the events-based pricing model would be a beneficial win-win not just for Amazon but for customers.

Today, AWS offers users a pay-as-you-go approach for pricing for over 200 cloud services. With AWS, users pay only for the individual services they need, for as long as they use them, and without requiring long-term contracts or complex licensing. AWS pricing is similar to how users pay for utilities like water and electricity. They only pay for the services they consume. Once they stop using the services, there are no additional costs or termination fees.

Results quickly validated the update to AWS's pricing model. The new pricing model perfectly aligned with AWS's target customer—developers who aren't keen on paying a cent more than they need for service. Thanks to its ability to better leverage its resources, AWS is now the largest cloud services operation in the world. *Forbes Magazine* predicts AWS could be a $1 trillion business by 2030.

A number of years ago, we were working with a technology company that had a wide range of products, some of them custom high-value products, others rock bottom commodities. The marketing manager for one product told us how one of their major customers had sent the company jet to pick up their monthly allocation of the product. Wow, what was going on in this business when a commodity was suddenly being treated as a high-value product? We suggested that the tech company raise its prices. They rejected this idea because prices were under contract. Yes, but the delivery times, we pointed out, were not similarly guaranteed.

The company took advantage of this reality by introducing a new product that was available immediately from stock at a 60% premium over the product that was taking 16 weeks to deliver. The customer's response was, "We wondered when you were going to figure out what was going on in this business." No complaints, just gratitude for having parts available.

The trick is to use price to fill capacity but to do it in a way that keeps the high-value customers paying fair but high prices and prevents them from wanting to take advantage of the low-value offering. And you want to make sure you don't let a low-value customer bump a high-value one.

Three Differentiated Pricing Plans

To make such value pricing work, managers need to adopt three differentiated pricing plans to manage capacity as shown in Figure 10.1. Each one is based on the utilization of the resources of the company. It is useful to think of each approach as being in a zone of utilization.

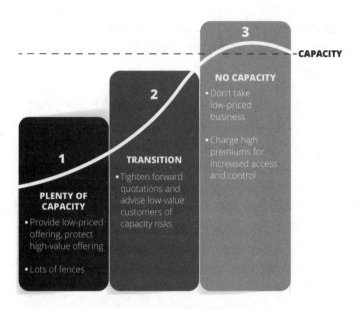

FIGURE 10.1 Using Price to Control Utilization

Zone 1 in Figure 10.1 represents the period when there is ample capacity. What many companies do during these periods is reduce the price of their high-value products. By doing so, they undermine the value structure of the company and their credibility with customers when the business cycle improves. Instead, the company should introduce low-value products or reduce service levels from the high-value package in order to protect the prices of the high-value offering.

Zone 2 is the transition period. When there are signs that the business is beginning to get busy, let the low-value customers know they might not get their products when they expected them. Make sure the expectation is set with these customers ahead of time. These customers believed they could get some products and services for low prices and are now disappointed that they can't. Remind them that they have choices: pay for the premium product that comes with premium delivery, pay for expedited delivery on an ad hoc basis, or accept a delay.

In Zone 3, the company is running at or above capacity. Don't waste a lot of time on most RFPs. Your main goal should be meeting existing customer demand. In fact, don't even bid on the low-priced opportunities because now there is a need to reserve capacity to satisfy high-value customers. Think about how airlines reserve some first-class seats for last-minute travelers. Always have a little extra capacity to take on the real high-value business, whether it be through an extra shift or weekend work. Costs will be a little higher, but the company should be charging a premium for customers to get capacity access during these times.

Companies can price based on capacity in any industry that has cycles of constraints and cost structures that are or can contribute to the capacity dynamic. Many industries, from professional services to steel and pulp and paper industries do this in a reactive manner by reducing prices on high-value products and services. They leave significant amounts of money on the table by not being initiative-taking about managing the capacity process and introducing low-value services and products with long lead times.

One industry segment that should use opportunity costing to control utilization is the professional services. Leaders here tend to look at their labor as a high variable cost when, in many cases, their costs are actually fixed. That is, the core group of people who are protected from any layoffs are a fixed cost and should therefore be viewed that way in both the costing and the pricing process.

Service firms tend to drop prices on high-value services and lose money. The Give-Get is to offer lower prices but to make sure some level of service and support is taken out of the offering.

By focusing on the value that professional resources bring to clients and learning to continually improve value, professional services companies are able to move out of the cost-based meat grinder of customer negotiations and into the value-based discussion with client executives that results in more benefit to everyone involved.

More Effective Give-Gets

Here's one more possibility that some of our clients find intriguing because it leads to better capacity utilization and higher profits. It calls for you to insert a clause in your sales contracts that gives you the right to "bump" certain customers when it becomes clear that you are at full capacity. The airlines do this kind of bumping all the time. While federal law gives them that right, we are all aware of how much passengers resent it. For you, that "magic clause" becomes a bargaining chip to use in price negotiations with procurement people. It becomes perhaps the most effective Give-Get to use in contract negotiations, and exercise it based on the three phases of capacity utilization shown in Figure 10.1.

Rather than having your salespeople always negotiating with price, they negotiate with the clause. When a procurement person asks for a lower price, the salesperson says, "No problem, but we have to have the right to bump you for our higher paying customers." To that, what will a typical poker-playing purchasing agent do? They'll pretend to get upset, which is a tell that they were playing poker all along.

The magic clause is another way the airlines stay profitable. It has application in a wide range of industries. Note the brute force method that UPS recently used during a recent peak holiday period. They charged Amazon $2 to $8 per package for the extra handling. UPS well understood that Amazon is trying to ramp up its own delivery infrastructure and that it was using UPS services to manage the packages they couldn't manage themselves. This understanding gave UPS enormous pricing leverage.

The current supply problems in the semiconductor industry have led to production problems in a wide range of industries, but none have been hurt worse than automobile producers. These hard-charging price buyers are suddenly faced with a shortage of computer chips. The shortage of these chips, which often cost less than $10 per unit, are holding up the production and sales of $40,000 automobiles. The procurement teams at the car makers have transitioned to poker playing in order to get supply at lower costs. Smart suppliers will invoke this clause in order to charge dramatically higher prices for their chips. We told the story of the chip maker that had a customer show up at the local airport in their corporate jet to take possession. The car maker was happy to pay a surcharge of 60% above to take reliable supply.

CHAPTER 11

Conclusion

Price with Confidence: The Journey

Customers buy results, not rhetoric. Moving beyond the rhetoric of value will enable you to demonstrate measurable results to customers. By applying 10 actionable rules, you can have confidence in your pricing decisions. In short, you will have cultivated Backbone. Now you can work with the salesforce to move the negotiation to a conversation of how you provide measurable results for customers. With confidence, your company will earn more profits and revenue by capturing the money currently being left on the table. All this won't happen overnight, but if you diligently apply the lessons of this book, these benefits will become real.

Who owns value? The ultimate answer, of course, is "everyone." The paradox, of course, is that when "everyone" is responsible for a resource, the practical effect is that no one is responsible. Most of the firms that engage our price strategy services have succumbed to some level of loss of profit accountability. Whatever the reason the firm surmises to be a core business issue, it's this loss of focus on value and accountability at the most senior levels that is at the heart of the problem.

When it comes to the central question of who owns value, the goal is for everyone in the organization to respond, emphatically, "I do!" Everyone in the value chain—everyone who designs, produces, or consumes the product or services—must own a piece of the resulting value. But individual action is not enough. The organization must develop a structural response to support individual action. To make pricing with confidence more than just an aspiration—to make it a sustainable presence in the organization, processes must be put in place to integrate the goals of individuals, departments, business units, and the enterprise as a whole into a cohesive go-to-market plan, offering by offering. We argue that without a sustained focus on developing this systematized value process by senior leaders, talking about pricing with confidence is meaningless rhetoric that quickly becomes a program of the month, ignored at the end of the quarter when a company needs to make its sales goals.

Why Most Companies Fail

Competitive advantage is more elusive than ever. To implement customer value recommendations and see the benefits of revenue and profit growth, we invite you to apply the principles set forth in this book. Putting any of the ten rules into practice and building structural norms to enforce them across the organization requires change. Change is not easy, and never more so than when it comes to shifting an organization's evolved pricing culture. We recently met with the CEO of a high-tech company we first assisted a number of years ago. During the meeting, the CEO said, "I've always wondered why your stuff never had any traction here." The answer was simple. First, there was only one person on his senior staff, our sponsor, who believed in the approach. It was a start, and it worked where it was tried, but the approach was never institutionalized as a team sport across all sectors of the enterprise.

Early on, the executive sponsor diligently applied the ten rules we outlined in this book to close the company's biggest and most profitable customer to date. The company successfully took on one of the toughest poker-playing purchasing agents in the industry and prevailed. The salespeople representing the product believed in the price because not only did they know the price was justified by the much higher value than the competitor's solution but could measure and demonstrate the difference. The sales teams appreciated getting real pricing power when they negotiated with tough customers. They successfully closed a $100 million dollar order that swept over $13 million into the company's coffers. But the CEO never supported or believed in the process and kept discounting prices to the demise of the entire 34,000-person organization.

Yes, But We Need to Meet the Numbers

As business managers, we learn to set financial objectives and then drive the people in the business to meet those numbers. That's what our bosses expect. That's what the analysts expect. There are a number of problems associated with driving employees to meet financial or other objectives, especially if meeting short-term goals is allowed to eclipse long-term objectives.

What happens if the results start coming up short of projections? Let's back up a step. When goals are set for the corporation, they trickle down to the divisions, business units, and regions. These projections are based on guesswork. Managers prefer the term assumptions. The assumptions take the form of forward-looking estimates about interest rates, prices of raw materials, energy costs, manufacturing capacity, and distribution logistics. The assumptions also factor in the behavior of competitors. All these numbers are crunched, and the resulting spreadsheets are quite impressive.

But managers can't have much confidence in assumptions driven by variables that are, by definition, uncontrollable and unpredictable. So managers consider the one resource that they can control: their salesforce. Many business forecasts are driven by assumptions about the salesforce's ability to deliver the numbers the managers promise. There are two critical problems with this reality. First, most managers typically overestimate their ability to get salespeople to deliver specific outcomes. The second problem is even more destructive. The business loses sight of what should be its main goal: delivering long-term value for its customers. Instead, its focus shifts to meeting numbers to keep managers and investors happy.

The Fool's Game of Price Competition

Price competition is a fool's game because any fool can play it. In fact, weak competitors have an advantage in price competition because they've got little to lose and nothing else to leverage. New entrants to the market also tend to use low price because they haven't yet proved their value to customers. Customers have discovered how to use price competition to their advantage. Customers qualify the low-priced vendors in order to get the high-value competitors to match the price.

Businesses are not always aware that they have been trapped. We got an urgent telephone call from the VP of sales of a well-known electronics company. He wanted our advice on the best price strategy for a reverse auction in which the company was participating. A reverse or procurement auction is often used in industrial business-to-business procurements. It is a type of auction in which the role of the buyer and seller are reversed, with the primary objective to drive purchase prices downward. In a conventional auction, buyers compete to obtain goods or services. In a reverse auction, sellers compete to obtain business.

We had but one question for the VP of sales: Was his company the preferred buyer? The answer was no. Our advice was to get out of the auction. It was a waste of time for the company. There was no possibility of the company winning the order. In this scenario, the company was a rabbit. Its only role was to pressure the two preferred vendors to drop their prices.

What should the company have done instead? Our advice was to use the bid request as an opportunity to visit the company and talk to the engineering team or real decision maker about value. As for the two preferred vendors, they were trapped, too. Without knowing the identity of the third vendor, they would be operating at a significant disadvantage when the rabbit dropped its price.

Customers who switch to you for price will be the first to leave when another low-price competitor comes along. Price competition provides no sustainable competitive advantage unless it can lead a firm to take over an industry and only in the high-growth phase of a life cycle.

The Customer Is All Powerful

"The customer is always right." We all know that adage. (We prefer an updated version that says, "The customer is all powerful.") The idea behind the original adage was that the customer is always in the best position to define their requirements. Well, it wasn't true in the twentieth century, and it's certainly not true in the twenty-first. The greatest new products rarely flowed in response to articulated customer requirements. No customer told Xerox to build the copy machine. But Xerox took a risk and identified a market that few customers envisioned. No customer asked Sony to build a battery-operated product smaller than a wallet to play music. But Sony built the Walkman and only then did customers recognize its benefits. And even more recently,

Apple repeated the same dynamic with the iPod. Customers were happy with Apple building computers. No one looked to it for managing and storing digital music. Today, Apple derives more revenues from converged consumer devices than from computers. In January 2007, the company dropped the word Computer from its legal name.

Here's the lesson. Customers may not always be right, but they are always powerful. It's important to know the difference. It's especially important to know the difference when considering what customers expect from pricing. Over the years, customers have learned that if they ask for a lower price, they will get it. In fact, customers have adopted an extensive list of tricks to get vendors to lower prices and then lower them again.

When customers ask for discounts, salespeople should turn the discussion to value. Customers expect this and typically attempt an end run on the salesperson. The customer telephones a senior manager at the salesperson's organization to rattle their cage in an attempt to get the manager to buy into the White Horse Syndrome. Sometimes the senior manager saves the customer the trouble by initiating the call. In either case, salespeople learn that when they try to hold the line on price, someone else in the organization will criticize them for messing up the sales opportunity. Salespeople quickly learn that they would be foolish to try to get additional profit for the company with higher prices. After all, aren't they paid to close deals, regardless of the costs for the company?

The challenge is getting salespeople and managers to have more confidence in their price. This requires salespeople and managers alike to resist undermining prices with short-term, panic-oriented tactics. The unwelcome news is that most companies do exactly that. The good news is that it takes just a few simple rules to reverse the habit, build discipline into the pricing process, and stop leaving money on the table.

The Journey

We are fortunate to have collaborated with many companies during their commercial transformation. To succeed, all companies start by improving every process critical to business success:

- Create a well-defined vision of what the future will be based on an assessment of the real opportunity.
- Understand why customers need your firm specifically (as opposed to a competitor). Value derives from that understanding.
- Negotiate with the value proposition. Doing so instills in customers a reason to buy and encourages sales professionals to have confidence in the value they provide.
- Set prices fairly given that perceived value is always relative to competitors. That means no less fair to your stakeholders than fair to the customer.
- Build trust. It's often the case that your customers buy because they trust you. That trust goes both ways and is part of the value you offer.

Start with Trust

Few readers will need to be convinced that upwards of 70% of all organizational change efforts fail, go over budget, take longer than expected, or deliver less than promised. Books have been written on why change is so difficult. Our takeaway is that of all the must-have elements of successful change efforts, the most critical is trust. On the most fundamental level, if the people in an organization cannot trust their leaders, at best they simply won't buy-in to the change. At worst, they will sabotage the effort. It's key that leaders cultivate a culture of trust before, during, and after a change effort if they expect the change initiative to meet any of the objectives set for it.

Everyone in the organization needs to trust that the price vision is an achievable one. That goal can be met only if the sales professionals had some buy-in to the development of the vision. Moreover, the vision must be simple to understand and simple to explain. If you can't explain the vision so a sixth-grader can understand it, it's too complicated. Nothing erodes trust in a proposed change more than foggy complexity.

When you embrace change as a mindset, only then can you begin the process of becoming a better pricer, manager, and leader. Part of that change entails believing that unearned discounting will rarely deliver the revenue and profitability results you want. Finally, you will learn that once you abandon habitual discounting, revenue and profits become goals that are actually possible to attain.

Our experience is that a lack of trust in the program translates into a lack of trust in the leaders promoting it. The only solution is to do a deep dive to figure out what the objections are. It's critical to create a process that surfaces the real objections, not just the stated ones. Ask for the objections. Remember that in this case, complaints are a gift. Only when you understood the objections can you design a program to address them. Here are some ideas to help build trust:

- Walk the walk. That's number one. Do what you say you're going to do. Too many times sales professionals have been promised this or that is definitely going to change and then follow-through never materializes. Too many times they have received reassurances of resources only to find the promises hollow. Do what you say you are going to do . . . that reliability is a key element of building trust.
- Make the vision real with simple data and track progress on the data often and rigorously.
- Hold people accountable, starting with the senior executives.

Nothing demoralizes teams more than a lack of accountability for failure. The best performers in any team will quickly leave if they are forced to work with subpar teammates.

- Reward the people who perform well. Recognition is critical, and not just with money.
- Root out and separate the nay-sayers.

This last bullet deserves elaboration. The time for protests is when the program is being designed. Protest must stop when the program is launched. Membership in an organization requires buy-in to legitimate business goals. If team members cannot accept the program, you must question their continued belonging in the organization. If individuals don't see the need to do that, leaders must ask them tough questions about buy-in, and, if necessary, separate them from the team.

Focus on Customer Experience

Learn what it's like to be a customer of your organization. Regular conversations with customers will be eye-opening. Here are two open-ended questions:

1. What's it like to do business with our company? Probe for good and bad. Ask for specifics.
2. Why do you continue to do business with our company and what impact is it making for you?

By the way, try to have these conversations with non-customers, as well.

Remember, this is not the time to turn the conversation into a sales call. They must be discovery conversations. Avoid any hint of sales or persuasion. In fact, if the customer you are interviewing gets even a whiff that they are being sold, they will rightfully resent the bait-and-switch.

Mark James holds the title of executive vice president for pricing and products for a department coordinating pricing for a €25 billion division of a global firm headquartered in Europe. Mark has a growth mindset and believes in moving his team forward. When he is persuaded that a novel approach has benefits, he deliberately introduces it to his team and invests in the training required to lead to its enterprise-wide adoption. Mark drove the adoption of Backbone for the sales team. When we recently asked him how his organization was managing the challenges of inflation, Mike emphasized that the support of the CEO was crucial to maintaining their pricing discipline. The company, Mark told us, would weather the inflation challenge fine because of these three practices:

- Passing on fuel price increases to customers via fuel surcharges, which became a global industry standard (aka, all competitors followed).
- Increasing other transportation costs in the form of a peak "emergency" fee. Competitors followed this step, as well.
- Adopting an annual price increase pegged to inflation.

Mark pointed out that he has learned to negotiate hard but fairly with his largest customers to the benefit of the enterprise. Over the years, he and his pricing team have added over 15% of margin to the company, representing €3.7 billion straight to the bottom line. We hope Mark got a big raise for that because he earned it. Mark is representative of the benefits that accrue when leaders adopt a mindset of change and are willing to get their entire global team on the value journey.

Our most successful client, a partner really, has been working to price with confidence for the past seven years. He had the sense that one of the new products that he inherited, and was being given away by other divisions to help them secure business, actually delivered unrecognized value. Working with the leadership team, we soon discovered that not only was there high value to the customer but a strong potential for more. Tough battles had to be fought inside and outside of the corporation to charge for this product.

Tough poker-playing negotiations ensued. Our partner won internally and now captures explicit value, creating billions of dollars of shareholder value. High stakes at the time. It took time, a strong vision, and the willingness to change, but over our time, the leadership team has coalesced to move from a sleepy division to a multi-billion-dollar powerhouse of revenue and profit growth for the enterprise.

Turbulent Times

Throughout much of this book, we've recommended ways to deal with the current turbulence: inflation, supply chain volatility, labor shortages, among other factors. Our main emphasis has been nimbleness and speed. But as Pricers, we've also got to think about supply excess and shortage, recession as well as inflation. We've got to have a broad view of our markets and not only the traditional factors such as customer segmentation, product differentiation, and evolving competition, but we also must have a wary eye and sufficient indicators to prepare for existing and potential turbulent times.

As the Fed increases interest rates to cool off demand and control inflation, there is a high probability that the market could go into a recession. So, what should companies do to prepare for such an occurrence?

"Stop the bleeding" should be a high priority in a recession. Controlling unnecessary costs gives the flexibility to choose from a variety of strategies as dictated by market forces. Not doing this will limit what you can do to stay profitable through a tough market.

Offering less value for your customers sounds counter-intuitive, but it can be an effective strategy during a recession since end-customers are often looking to reduce costs by moving to low-cost products. Understanding how best to reduce value to retain customers is critical for long-term profitability. Just giving customers the ability to make that choice will solidify your relationship. In addition, this new flanking product strategy may allow companies to enter new markets that they have not played in historically. The strategy starts with an understanding of what customers in this segment "need to have" and what offerings are "nice to have." Success depends on concentrating on the former.

Companies that thrive during a recession often are the ones that find ways to create new sources of value. One example is by partnering with other companies in the channel to bring an integrated solution to the end-customer. End-customers tend to be risk averse during a recession, which creates new opportunities for companies that can be nimble enough to meet their needs as markets change.

This gets us to our final piece of advice, and we feel that this is the most important. Before we give it, know that we trained on and use some of the most sophisticated statistical techniques out there, but we have learned that it's easy to get lost in the complexity of those techniques.

We avoid the complexity of the techniques as well as the difficulty of modeling your markets. Complex spreadsheets and analysis have to, at some point, boil down to simple insights that lead to simple conclusions. Complexity just gets in the way of that. Simplicity works because everyone understands it and is likely to, pricing or otherwise, be able to exercise it with confidence. Boeing, Southwest Airlines, and Apple have learned this approach and, despite the complexity of their products and operations, have executed with simple strategies that everyone can understand.

This is especially true for pricing. The problem is that is usually takes an ability to rise above the complexity and present the complexity in simple terms so that people can understand it. Some clients feel the need to see evidence of complexity, so give it to them in an appendix. If you do that, clients will trust that you've done your homework and that your proposals are supported by research.

The pricing approach (UVPF) that this book encourages is best supported with simple constructs. Concepts such as understanding value and pricing fairly needn't be complicated. It's a misguided effort that confuses complexity with rigor and just confuses stakeholders. How many definitions of value are there? Complex value calculations may be impressive on a whiteboard but never get implemented. The concepts that actually work are the ones that can be represented on the back of a napkin.

Communicating a basic understanding of value is critical to giving sales teams the confidence to defend the price, which is simply the representation of that value. Communication is the act of the recipient. Complexity undermines communication. The knowledge of the application of your products and services, its subsequent value, and your ability to simplify the process is key to success. Simplicity better leverages and provides a return of growing revenue and profits. Once an organization internalizes those truths, its search for value will be complete.

About the Authors

Dr. Reed K. Holden, founder of Holden Advisors, is a world-class pricing expert who helps clients build go-to-market strategies to drive price leadership, Selling Backbone, and profitable growth. Dr. Holden specializes in helping sales and pricing teams avoid the Procurement Buzz Saw by implementing value strategies to recognize and counter margin reducing buying tactics. He is an enthusiastic and persuasive advocate for demonstrating customer value and price leadership with companies that need to adapt in highly competitive markets.

In 2012, Dr. Holden published *Negotiating with Backbone: Eight Strategies to Defend Your Price and Value*, and in 2008, with co-author Mark Burton, he published *Pricing with Confidence: Ten Ways to Stop Leaving Money on the Table*, a top-selling pricing book for the executives. He also co-wrote *The Strategy and Tactics of Pricing* second and third editions during his tenure as CEO of Strategic Pricing Group (now Monitor|Deloitte).

A dynamic and provocative presenter with over 25 years of experience, Dr. Holden keynotes at executive and sales events for Fortune 1000 companies. Organizations that strive for price leadership engage Dr. Holden Reed to provide B2B pricing and negotiating advice to entities building go-to-market strategies to drive price leadership, Selling Backbone and profitable growth. Reed is married with two children, three grandchildren, and two dogs, and resides in Concord, Massachusetts.

Jeet Mukherjee, vice president of Pricing at Holden Advisors, specializes in hardware and software pricing with a B2B focus. Armed with over two decades worth of global experience in management consulting, strategy, analytics, marketing, and pricing, Jeet left the Fortune 100 world to help clients defend their value through pricing at Holden Advisors. As a pricing expert,

Jeet has presented in multiple conferences across the nation and the world, and taught executives from startups to Fortune 100 companies.

He holds an MBA from Boston University's Questrom School of Business and has worked with clients in distribution, pharmaceutical, healthcare, and technology sectors. He is also the proud recipient of an Edelman Laureate for his work in business analytics and optimization within distribution.

Jeet lives in Phoenix with his wife, Kelly, their two sons, Aidan and Kyle, and their dogs, Ozzie and Hudson.

About Holden Advisors

Based in Concord, Massachusetts, Holden Advisors is a global team of experts in pricing and sales performance. We'll help you take control of your differential value and use it to transform your business. We help commercial teams quantify business value, mitigate risk, and go to market faster—the essentials of improving profit performance. By aligning your commercial organization around the value of your solution, you can offer a fair price relative to competitors and show clients results others have received using the solution. And increase both your revenue and profits. In more than 30 years of working with Fortune 500 corporations, venture-backed start-ups, and a variety of entrepreneurial organizations around the world, we've developed a proficiency in pricing and sales performance that few others can match. For more information, visit www.holdenadvisors.com.

Index